THE HOLOCAUST WARS

THE OPINIONS/CRITIQUES/RESEARCH BOOKS

Written By: Jacob Sternberg ("JS")

With Significant Assistance by:

Jacob Gostl ("JG")

And: Christina Sternberg ("CTS")

© Project Gideon Company, 2023

THE OPINIONS/CRITIQUES/RESEARCH BOOKS

Selected by the Author

From PGC Knowledge Base

A Book In Two Volumes:

Volume 1   Controversial Opinions

© Project Gideon Company, 2023

The Holocaust Wars Project - Books to be published in 2023

Jacob's Odyssey – The Early Years
Jacob's Odyssey – Coming to America
The Applicants for Sainthood
The Troller Wars
The Holocaust Wars – Opinions
The Holocaust Wars – Critiques and Presentations
The Ride on America's Business Highway
Winning – A Play
The Khelm Revolutions
The Rabbi from Khelm
The Holocaust Wars – Excerpts/Treatments

Visit PGC's website for books availability.
https://www.projectgideoncompany.com

© Project Gideon Company, 2023

Dedication

This book is dedicated to Professor Ben-Cion Pinshuk, my lifelong friend with whom I debated mundane and important issues over seven decades.

A most honorable mensch.

© Project Gideon Company, 2023

VOLUME I
CONTROVERSIAL OPINIONS

ROADMAP

I.1 The Holocaust - Summary/Singularity/Business Mode..............1
   Written by Christina Sternberg

I.2 The Role of Psychiatry in the Holocaust 32
   Written by Jacob Gostl

I.3 They Didn't Just Go Quietly – Uprisings................................58
   Written by Jacob Gostl

I.4 What is Unique About the Holocaust Events..........................76
   Written by Jacob Sternberg

I.5 The Questions Not Asked and Answers Not Given 112
   Written by Jacob Sternberg

I.6 The Rancher's Rant... 156
   Written by Jacob Sternberg

© Project Gideon Company, 2023

VOLUME I CONTROVERSIAL OPINIONS

© Project Gideon Company, 2023

VOLUME I. CONTROVERSIAL OPINIONS

I.1   THE HOLOCAUST

The Holocaust is unique in the history of mankind.

It is a tragedy of unprecedented scope perpetrated

by a brutal totalitarian regime –

the Nazis' attempt to eradicate the Jewish people.

The so-called "Final Solution" mandated

the annihilation of every Jew in the world.

AUTHOR'S NOTE

The views expressed herein are mine; the content is not intended as a substitute for standard references, accounts of survivors, historical analytical works or other authoritative documentation.

I am not a professional historian, I am trained and experienced as an information scientist, qualified at organizing, classifying, abstracting and documenting technical materials. I have spent decades of my professional career in information management at GE's Atomic Installations, CBS, Shell Oil and my husband's high-tech companies.

© Project Gideon Company, 2023

I.1 "THE HOLOCAUST" OPINION

I.1.1 Summary 3

I.1.2 A Singular Event 9

I.1.3 A Nazi Business Model 22

I.1.1 SUMMARY

The Holocaust stands apart for many reasons:

- Throughout World War II ("WWII"), the Nazi regime was not only conducting military campaigns in Europe, Russia and Africa, and carrying out advanced research projects in weaponry and rocketry – but also frantically endeavoring to complete the Final Solution.

    "Between 1941 and 1945, murdering the Jews was as great a priority for Hitler as winning WWII, if anything, greater." ("Rabbi Joseph Telushkin, "Jewish Literacy" p. 347).

- Hitler didn't want just some Jews, or even many Jews killed – he wanted all Jews killed. And the process had to be carried out neatly and efficiently. Large scale executions couldn't be done in populous area; that would have been too disruptive. Mass shootings were done, but generally in less populated areas.

    The insidious use of gas chambers allowed the Nazis to simultaneously murder many very quickly in a hands-off manner, they left the dirty work of disposal to Slavs who were treated as slave labor and to Jews who were subsequently killed. The Nazis didn't want living witnesses to their crimes.

- That Jews were tormented, degraded, stripped of all value – material worth and humanizing qualities – before being killed is the crux of Nazi horror.

    No other dictator, tyrant, regime in modern history has been animated by such obsessive, ruthless, murderous hatred aimed at a specific segment of its population – not Stalin in the Russian gulags, not Mao with his cultural revolution in China, not Pol Pot in Cambodia.

- Although the focus is on Hitler – commonly shown as Der Führer rousing thousands to Sieg Heil salutes, -- as the megalomaniac leader of the Third Reich, responsibility for the Holocaust is not his alone.

  Hitler's hatred of Jews was known to Germans before he became Chancellor in 1933; once in power, his antisemitic actions began almost immediately.

  The entire German society, led by its intelligentsia, willingly endorsed the policies, and readily collaborated with the operations of the Nazi regime. The civilization that valued intellectual and cultural achievement – the land of Mozart, Beethoven, Goethe, Durer, Freud, Einstein – was corrupted by rabid, irrational antisemitism.

- The most demonic criminality of the Nazi regime was without doubt against Jewish children. A death sentence was near certain for infants and young children.

  Older teens who were captured and were capable of hard work had a slight chance of survival, if luck was on their side.

  Children sent to the Theresienstadt concentration camp had virtually no chance of survival – "… because they represented the Jewish future, children were among the earliest to die." (Michael Berenbaum "In Memory's Kitchen, p. xiii). After a short stay in Theresienstadt, they were re-deported to death camps. A telling a grim statistic: Of the 15,000 children sent to the Theresienstadt camp, only 100 survived at the end of the war (0.6%).

- In defeat, the Nazis did not express remorse or guilt. If anything, they were only sorry not to have finished the job they set out to do.

After the war, many Nazis escaped to welcoming countries where they lived comfortably the rest of their days on stolen Jewish wealth.

The pre-war Jewish population of Europe was concentrated mostly in Central and Eastern Europe (Poland, Germany, Hungary, Rumania, Ukraine, Belarus, etc.). Jews with foresight and/or resources who emigrated before 1939 were fortunate. Once the war started, Jews in Nazi-controlled areas faced a terrifying future.

The possibilities for survival were dire and limited:

- Attempt to flee to a country that would accept them as refugees.

- Try to go into hiding or find sanctuary somewhere deemed safe, such as a church.

- Be confined in a ghetto, labor camp, or otherwise under rigid Nazi surveillance; or be imprisoned in a concentration camp.

By late 1939, German military forces were in control of Austria and Czechoslovakia, had conquered Poland, and were advancing on all fronts across Europe.

The following is a true account of what happened to six family members, ordinary individuals who became extraordinary because of WWII and the Holocaust.

IN JANUARY 1940:

In January 1940, in the early days of World War II:

- Ester, a 22-year-old Jewish nurse's aide, escaped with her baby son from the Warsaw ghetto hidden in a garbage truck. Her feet were stabbed by Nazi soldiers searching the refuse with their bayonets.

- Jacob, Ester's baby, just a year-and-a-half old, had to quickly learn that his and his mother's survival depended on his absolute obedience. To be anything but silent and uncomplaining could jeopardize their lives.

- Eliezer, Ester's husband and Jacob's father, a young Jewish university lecturer, was in a part of Russian-controlled Poland, hoping to reunite with his wife and child, uncertain when – or if – they would find each other.

- Chaim, a 31-year-old Polish Jew who was a candy maker by trade, was fighting against the Nazis with a band of Jewish partisans in the Polish woods.

- Dr. Theodor Troller I ("TTI"), a 76-year-old widowed country doctor in Czechoslovakia, designated a "Privileged Jew" by the Nazis, was being persecuted by their relentless application of the Nuremberg Laws, while dealing with burst pipes and loss of indoor plumbing caused by the frigid temperatures of an unusually harsh winter.

- Theodor Troller II, the son of Dr. Troller I, a 36-year-old, world class scientist with his doctorate in aeronautical engineering from a top German university, had been recruited in 1931 by his former professor (the preeminent aerodynamicist Theodor von Karman, "Father of the Space Age") to head the Guggenheim Airship Institute in Akron, Ohio; he was heavily engaged in the American war effort, using his aeronautics expertise and inventiveness in high-level business and government projects.

IN MAY 1945:

In May 1945, by the end of the war in Europe:

- Ester had lost her husband, her mother, her siblings, her friends, her home, her possessions. After three years in Russia, she was in Poland with Jacob and a younger son born during the war, preparing to start a new life, destination unknown. She was 27.

- Jacob had lost his father; he had lost his childhood; he remembered only hunger, cold, and fear. Just short of his seventh birthday, he was a very quiet, serious boy with a keen awareness of what had actually happened.

- Eliezer had lost his life in 1945. He died in an accident of unknown cause in a Russian munitions factory. He was probably in his late twenties when he died.

- Chaim had lost his family, including a wife and young children, his home, his livelihood. Sometime near the end of the war, Chaim married Ester and became Jacob's stepfather, giving Jacob his last name.

- Theodor Troller I had lost his life in 1944. He died in the Theresienstadt concentration camp, three hours before orders arrived for his transport to Auschwitz. He was 80 years old.

- Theodor Troller II had lost his father in Theresienstadt; his aunts and cousins in Auschwitz; and, most profoundly and life-altering, a world view that had informed his entire being. The German culture of intellectual achievement and refinement that was his foundation and he had revered was desecrated irreparably by the Nazis.

By the war's end, every U.S. ship and every U.S. plane was provided with his patented inventions. Given the rank of Colonel, he was in Europe on a classified military mission to interview and recruit German scientists and technologists in all technical and scientific disciplines of potential use to America.

It is not possible to describe adequately, especially in abbreviated form, the magnitude, the scope, the sheer perversity of the Holocaust.

I have concentrated on what I consider most basic to understanding why the Nazi evil has left such an indelible imprint on history.

In writing about what I believe defines the uniqueness of the Holocaust, I use the words singular and singularity. It is terminology that in my opinion most accurately conveys the unprecedented, incomparable nature of what the Nazis did.

I.1.2 A SINGULAR EVENT

The Holocaust is a singular event in human history. It is an incomprehensible tragedy; the Nazis attempt to annihilate the Jews. They succeeded in killing Six Million in Europe, and causing irreparable damage to the Jews who remained – those who had survived, those who had escaped, those anywhere who had watched helplessly and waited anxiously to learn the fate of family and friends. Profound, lifelong suffering was inflicted on the countless individuals, Jews and non-Jews alike, who had firsthand knowledge of what the Nazis did.

There are many who deny that the Holocaust ever happened. Deniers, or revisionists as they euphemistically call themselves, use their political narrative to mask what is in reality a malignant hatred of Jews.

There are many who minimize the Holocaust by calling it a genocide and grouping it with other large-scale massacres that occurred worldwide in the 20th Century, some with even greater casualties. But none is comparable to the Holocaust.

To say the Holocaust is like other mass killings is to cavalierly dismiss a brutal premeditated extermination carried out from 1938 to 1945 that was singular in purpose and singular in implementation.

The singularity derives from the ruthless totalitarian strategy that was diabolically conceived, meticulously planned, methodically executed by the highest caliber of German society. I believe the following elemental points describe how the Nazi regime systematically orchestrated, from start to finish, their hate-obsessed operation to murder Jews.

- <u>CONCEPT/PURITY OF BLOOD</u>

At the core of Nazi evil, as clearly and unequivocally stated in the Nuremberg Laws, was the belief "… that purity of German (Aryan) blood is the essential condition for the continued existence of the German people … for all time …" The purification could be achieved by exterminating all Jews. No other justification was required for the horror that followed.

In Hitler's view, Jews were evil incarnate; the only effective solution to the "Jewish problem" was to annihilate every Jew in the world. The name he chose for his program to murder all Jews was "The Final Solution to the Jewish Problem."

- **IDEOLOGY, RACE BASED**

Calling Jews a race allowed the Nazis to establish their own legal definition of Jewishness. The racial theories prevalent in Nazi ideology were institutionalized by the Nuremberg Laws enacted by the Reichstag (Germany's parliament) in 1935.

According to the Nazis, Jews were a race defined by birth and by blood, not by religious affiliation, i.e., what religion they did or did not practice, but by family genealogy. Individuals having three or four grandparents born into a Jewish religious community were, by law, Jewish. This was irrevocable, with no way to challenge or change, the designation; there was absolutely <u>no</u> personal choice in the matter.

The "racial" status assigned by the Nazis was passed to children and grandchildren.

Hatred of Jews was of central importance to the Nazi party. The Nuremberg Laws and subsequent legislation provided the legal framework for the systematic persecution of Jews in Germany.

Jews were deprived of German citizenship and considered "subjects" of the state. Policies and procedures were formulated to impoverish Jews (and enrich the Nazis) by "legitimately" confiscating Jewish businesses, property, and monetary assets in a process termed "Aryanizing." Strict limits were imposed on social rights, dictating whom Jews could and could not associate with. Prohibitions were imposed on German citizens as well; giving aid to Jews could result in severe punishment, even death.

- <u>**PROPAGANDA**</u>

Capitalizing on the theme of Jewish racial impurity, the Nazis embarked on a highly-effective psychological campaign to incite virulent Jew-hatred in the German population. Harassing, attacking, terrorizing Jews was encouraged and without consequence. The Nazi regime condoned antisemitic acts by German citizens. By not prosecuting crimes against Jews, by not making them illegal acts, the Nazis were essentially legalizing antisemitic behavior.

This culminated in the violent rampages throughout Germany of Kristallnacht (November 9-10, 1938), an all-out assault on Jewish homes, businesses, and synagogues. The largest pogrom in history, a well-coordinated race riot aimed at every Jew in Germany, it resulted in untold destruction of property, shattered windows in almost every German synagogue, and dead Jews, killed by lawless mobs.

Kristallnacht sealed the fate of German Jews, and clearly demonstrated that malignant Jew-hatred, fostered by the Nazi regime, was deeply embedded in German citizenry.

The Nazis were assured of continuous antisemitism that could be used to their advantage.

- <u>**COMPLIANCE**</u>

With unity of purpose – focus on the hatred of Jews – the Nazis readily coopted the entire German society into lockstep pursuit of their goals.

From participation of the military and its auxiliary functions, to the industrial complex to the transport sector, to legions of clerical staff, a large segment of the population was directly involved in support of Holocaust-related activities.

The judicial and legislative systems, academic institutions, science, medicine, the highest levels of intelligentsia all were willingly in compliance with Nazi antisemitic ideology.

This corruption extended as well to countries allied with or under Nazi control. By 1941, Italy, Hungary, Romania, Czechoslovakia, Bulgaria, Vichy France, Netherlands, Austria and Croatia had enacted anti-Jewish legislation similar to the Nuremberg Laws. In every European country conquered by the Nazis, legislation was passed that required Jews to wear a yellow star on their clothing.

- **DECEPTION**

The Nazis needed to camouflage the execution of what they knew was an inherently sinister and criminal plan. They were confronted with two issues: the Final Solution couldn't be completely achieved in a short period of time, and too many resources couldn't be diverted at once from military needs. The logistics problem of eliminating so many Jews spread over such a large area required deceptions to prevent panic and uprisings among the Jews, and to ensure compliant behavior in the German population.

The earliest and effective large-scale deception surrounded the 1936 Olympics held in Berlin. Because the Olympics were important for German prestige, and Hitler didn't want international criticism of his government, anti-Jewish attacks were moderated for a brief period. Signs on public places saying "Jews Unwelcome" were removed; nevertheless, German Jewish athletes were not allowed to participate in the games.

Under pressure, two Jewish runners on the American team were replaced by black athletes, showing that hatred of Jews took precedence over racial prejudice toward blacks.

A widespread deception was that Jews who were rounded up in groups or who simply disappeared were being "relocated" to the East; supposedly a better place to live. This was reiterated even when the reality was known.

After the war, much of the German population still maintained a pretense of "not knowing" – which, given the intensity and duration of the effort, was simply not credible, and by then, too many individuals and businesses were missing to feign such innocence.

An especially sadistic ruse to prevent panic in the death camps was telling Jews who were condemned to the gas chambers that they were being sent to showers – even giving them fake bars of soap.

Unlike other concentration camps, Theresienstadt was an elaborate hoax, set up as a "model" camp intended to show the world how well the Nazis were treating Jews, and to deflect unpleasant inquiries about the disappearance of well-known Jews; it was the destination for artists, musicians, writers, scholars, scientists, jurists, successful professionals, and other prominent Jews, including distinguished veterans from WWI.

In fact, conditions in Theresienstadt were so harsh, the camp was so disease-ridden with typhus and dysentery, the death rate was so high that a crematorium had to be built. Theresienstadt actually functioned as a waiting room for transport to the death camps, usually Auschwitz.

For a visit by the International Red Cross on June 23, 1944, which resulted from insistent demands by the Danish government for accountability about its citizens who had been sent to Theresienstadt in late 1943 – the camp was turned into a sham showplace. The Potemkin Village set included a band playing light music, a café filled with customers, a bank, stores with goods in the windows, a flower garden, even a soccer game; Danish inmates were in freshly painted rooms with two or three occupants instead of the usual three or found times that number. A children's opera, 'Brundibar," was performed for the guests.

"The deception succeeded so well that later a propaganda film was made at Theresienstadt showing how well the Jews were faring under the benevolent protection of the Third Reich. When the filming was over, most of the cast, including the children, was sent to Auschwitz." (Michael Berenbaum, Foreword to "In Memory's Kitchen" p. xiv)

Such was the duplicity of Theresienstadt, "The City Hitler Built for the Jews" as it was cynically referred to in Nazi propaganda. The world at large, knowing full well what was going on during the war for the most part looked the other way.

- **METHODOLOGY**

The Nazi regime was systematic, methodical, disciplined in implementing its lethal operations. Only the Nazis created death camps with gas chambers and crematoria designed for efficient mass extermination. From theory to practice, from inception to defeat, they carried out the Holocaust with unparalleled attention to detail.

German society in general valued hard work, efficiency, obedience, pedantic adherence to bureaucratic policies and procedures, qualities that were ingrained in their culture. Following rules to ensure good order was part of the Germanic ethos. In the Nuremberg trials, just following [the] orders [of my superior] was a standard defense tactic against the criminal charges.

The German language itself is a model of clarity and precision, noted for lengthy sentences with multisyllabic words that allow for exactness in verbal expression. The Nazis drew distinctions among Jews according to their percentage of Jewishness (based on number of grandparents), wealth and status, and religious affiliation of their marital partner. The term "Mischlinge" was coined to describe "mixed-race" individuals who were a quarter or half Jewish (one of two grandparents). A "Privileged Jew" (such as TTI) was a prominent or accomplished Jew. In early 1945, many thousands of Mischlinge and Jews who were married to non-Jews were deported to Theresienstadt and other camps in a desperate attempt by the Nazis to eliminate as many Jews as possible before war's end.

The penchant for bureaucrat's orderliness was manifested in the comprehensive record-keeping and documentation of the Nazi regime, from the precise wording of the Nuremberg Laws that initially codified the definition and treatment of Jews, to capturing every bit of available personal information on Jews.

For a Jew, the scrutiny was inescapable. The Nazis kept detailed data on family genealogy, marriage and birth records, addresses of homes and businesses, property ownership, bank accounts, deportation and transport orders, lists of concentration camp inmates, and of course deaths.

This was a mammoth undertaking, especially in the days before computers, requiring significant manpower dedicated to collecting, recording, filing, and retrieving information – it was done neatly, accurately, efficiently.

As an indication of their commitment to thoroughness in documentation, the Nazis even created a Judaica Museum in Prague as a repository for artifacts of the culture they intended to annihilate.

- <u>**ETHOS**</u>

    "The distinguishing character, sentiment, moral nature, or guiding beliefs of a person, group of institution."
    (Websters 9th New Collegiate History)

With their belief in Aryan superiority, the Nazis established a measure of worth for other humans. Non-Aryans were all inferior beings, but Jews were degraded to subhuman status – without question the ultimate cruelty in the Nazi arsenal of evils. With sadistic, obsessive calculation, the Nazis deprived Jews of political rights, personal choice, individuality, self-respect, dignity, and transformed them into hateful object of scorn.

From the obligatory wearing of the Star of David, which immediately singled out and stigmatized Jews, to transport in filthy, overcrowded cattle cars, to incarceration in the hell of concentration camps with shaved heads, tattooed identity numbers, worn lice-infested uniforms, the total loss of humanizing qualities was obscenity assured.

The Nazis used the term extermination to describe the murder of inmates in death camps, implying that it was not human beings who were being killed, but rats that were being "exterminated."

For Hitler, simply murdering the Jews was not sufficient. He wanted them tortured and humiliated as well. And the Nazis complied, whenever and however they could.

Jews were nothing more than exploitable commodities from which every bit of value and labor could be extracted.

They were a source of wealth for the Nazi regime, from whom all assets and belongings could be confiscated. They were a source of labor for German industrial production of munitions. In the camps, they toiled in subhuman conditions with starvation-level rations until they died; in death, their skin, fat, and gold teeth were salvaged, harvested.

Jews who were not yet captive in camps or ghettos had a monetary value for informants. By putting a bounty on Jews who were still at large in conquered countries, the Nazis encouraged citizens to actively hunt for them; the promise of reward money was a powerful incentive in Holland specially given the wartime scarcity of food and other necessities. Jews in hiding lived in constant terror of being discovered and turned over to the Nazis – by strangers, neighbors, even friends, anyone was potentially an informer.

Although Jews were most reviled and slated for total eradication, Nazi cruelty extended to other categories they deemed undesirable; individuals with mental and/or physical impairments, political dissidents, gypsies (Roma), and homosexuals were selectively imprisoned or murdered outright. Slavs, who were considered an inferior people, were exploited as a slave-labor force.

It is estimated that between 1933 and 1945 the Nazi regime and its allies established more than 44,000 camps and other incarceration sites, including ghettos, concentration camps, killing (euthanasia) centers, forced labor camps, transit camps, and prisoner-of-war camps.

Even when the war was over, the systemic brutality of the Nazis continued. "British troops were advancing on Neuengamme, [a labor camp in northern Germany.] Hitler had committed suicide a few days earlier, and SS Chief Heinrich Himmler had given orders not to surrender the camps with their prisoners. Guards put some 8,000 inmates onto two ships, the Cap Arcona and the Thielbeck. On May 3, a British Air Force squadron, knowing nothing about the ships' human cargo, bombed and sank them." El Paso Times, "Retracing a lost life." 12/18/06.

The Nazis knew that German warships would be certain targets for allied bombers.

One cannot say enough about the systemic brutality that defined the Nazi regime.

I.1.3 A NAZI BUSINESS MODEL

The Holocaust should be remembered not only for what was done, but also for how it was done. The Nazi regime put in place an operation that steadily, efficiently, ruthlessly killed an average of 2,900 Jews per day, over five and a half years (January 1940 – May 1945). Such an immense and widespread effort required massive logistical support. There was nothing haphazard or spontaneous or careless in how the Nazis conducted their extermination process: it was an all-encompassing, meticulously planned, rigorously administered, precisely executed operation, overseen by the highest-caliber Nazi officers.

The Nazis were so deliberate and so methodical in carrying out the Final Solution, they appeared to have created and followed the equivalent of a modern-day business model – though on an unimaginably vast scale. A contemporary business plan is the prerequisite for introducing a new corporate entity, product, or service; it describes in detail what the innovation is and how it will be introduced into the marketplace, and provides relevant financial information.

The format of business plans is variable, but generally a plan contains subject headings that cover: objective/mission; description of the innovation; management; marketing/sales; competition; risk factors; public relations; implementation/operations; financials (projected expenses, revenues, path to profitability); information management; and other topics deemed relevant. The overall content and order of a business plan are intended to optimize the chances for success of the undertaking.

That the Nazis appeared to follow an analogous approach can be surmised from their known actions and documentation. Based on the evidence, it is not difficult to imagine the Nazi version of a business plan. The essential information can be summarized using the subject headings outlined above.

Objective/Mission

As explicitly stated in the Nuremburg Laws, the Nazis' objective was to achieve purity of German blood as the essential condition to ensure continued existence of the German people for all time.

Innovation

The Nazi "innovation" was the formulation of the "Final Solution," the idea that all Jews must be eliminated to ensure the purification of German (Aryan) blood.

Management

The management team, led by CEO A. Hitler, consisted of top-level Nazi executives.

Marketing/Sales

Building on the antisemitism embedded in their ideology, the Nazis developed a marketing campaign, i.e., sophisticated propaganda, to "sell" the idea of Jew-hatred to the German people. This laid the groundwork for the continued compliance and cooperation of the entire society.

Competition

This was a totalitarian enterprise; by definition, there was no competition. Dissent of any sort was not allowed.

Risk Factors

Carrying out the Final Solution posed two serious, continuing risks for the Nazis: vital resources had to be diverted from military needs; and the criminality of their actions might be discovered. No direct orders for killing Jews have been found; orders apparently were transmitted in person to avoid the possibility of disclosures.

Public Relations

A public relations program was conducted throughout the war in an attempt to obscure reality and deflect questions about what was really happening. Three types of deception were needed: to prevent panic and resistance in the Jewish population; to ensure the continuing and full cooperation of German society; and to convince the world of Hitler's benign treatment of Jews and other non-Aryan "racial aliens" (blacks and Roma/Gypsies).

Note: Although the truth was known to many early in the war, the Nazis' deceptions were successful enough that there was never a slow down or interruption in the killing operations; and, in fact, there was actually an increase as the war was nearing its end.

Implementation

Implementing the Final Solution entailed a complex series of ongoing as well as one-time steps, each an enormous project in itself:

- Enact the legislation and issue ancillary decrees to provide the legal framework for the systematic persecution of Jews.

- Determine who is Jewish, with the designation of their type/level (full, Mischlinge, Privileged) using birth, marriage, and other records; issue identity cards and require all those inescapably labeled Jewish by the Nazi definition to carry the cards for easy identification by police.

- Define overall Final Solution operational requirements including schedules/phasing and resource allocation for facilities, manpower, transportation and other needs.

- Establish policies and procedures for administration, communications, monitoring/control and oversight of the various components and functions.

- Construct the system of physical structures and complexes for confining, imprisoning, and killing Jews, i.e., the concentration camps (with gas chambers and crematoria), transit camps, work camps, ghettos, etc., each with its own administrative and workforce needs.

Note: Once implementation was complete, the Final Solution system ran like clockwork, operating at full capacity throughout the war. New prisoners arrived regularly at the camps, rounded up from ghettos in conquered areas.

The ovens did not stand idle, and the work forces did not fall below required levels. Continuing cooperation between the military and industrial sectors was imperative, as the high death rate of workers due to starvation, illness, and mistreatment made constant replenishment of the slave labor necessary. The work done by prisoners was essential to the war effort.

Financials

Financing the Final Solution was a high priority for the Nazis. Standard business plan financial information includes expenses, revenues, and profits, and would have been covered in detail.

Jewish wealth was a significant and continuing source of income for the Nazis. It would likely have been categorized as potential (not yet appropriated or "Aryanized"), or already confiscated, and itemized by type: cash/bonds/stocks; pensions/insurance policies; residential properties; business merchandise and properties; jewelry; art; household valuables (silver, rugs), etc., etc., etc.

A major contribution to the Nazi revenue stream came from possessions taken from concentration camp prisoners before – and after – death, especially the gold from rings and teeth.

Information Management

The Nazis were clear about what to document; they kept meticulous and extensive records of their Holocaust activities. The amount of documentation amassed by the Nazis for their Final Solution operations is astonishing. Consider some of the types of records needed for their purposes, each category with entries for millions of Jews:

- Genealogical and other records used to determine Jewishness and issue identity cards to designated Jews.

- Any and all information relevant to Jewish wealth – bank accounts, pensions, residential and business property registrations, etc.

- Inventories of confiscated valuables (art, jewelry, etc.) and where stored.

- Death lists.

- Concentration camp registrations.

- Forced labor rolls/work camp registrations.

- Transit orders. This category alone had to include many millions of names (on individual forms and on lists), as individuals were routinely transported from shtetls and other sites to the various camps, and were frequently re-transported from camp to camp.

It should be remembered that the information management required by the Nazis was in an era when information had to be handwritten or typed (using a manual typewriter) on printed forms or blank sheets of paper. Information technology that today is taken for granted did not exist then – there were no computers, no copying machines, no fax machines, no advanced microfilm technology, no electric typewriters with error correction capability. Manual typewriters had keys that jammed and ink ribbons that had to be replaced; frugal typists saved money by using ribbons until the ink was barely legible. Making copies involved typing with two or three carbon sheets inserted between the paper, always a messy process.

There had to have been legions of clerks in countless offices to generate, organize, file, store, and retrieve the huge amounts of information – and to physically deliver information when and where it was needed. Procedures had to have been in place to maintain information flow, coordinate information from different sources, keep track of directives, control access to sensitive information, and overall manage the documentation.

This was a labor-intensive, time-consuming, resource-diverting effort, and yet the Nazis were insistent on their pedantic record keeping. They produced enough information to incriminate themselves, and to keep future generations of scholars quite busy.

Concluding Thoughts

Putting the Holocaust in the context of a business model makes readily apparent the enormity, the meticulousness, the obsessiveness of the Nazis' operation to kill Jews, even when they were losing on the military front. Which raises the question, why did the Nazis go to so much trouble, why did they expend so much time and effort to carry out such an elaborate, systematic atrocity? They could have simply done what other dictators/regimes did: use mass starvation or mass executions as a means of eliminating targeted segments of their population. With Jews incarcerated in large numbers in ghettos and camps, the Nazis could easily have poisoned food or water supplies, or used lethal gasses in enclosed areas. In the waning days of the war, they could have bombed the camps and claimed the Allies did it.

There were paradoxes in Nazi actions and behavior, in their demanding a mass-killing process that was premeditated, controlled, methodical. Though they carefully provided a legal framework for the merciless persecution of Jews and confiscation of Jewish wealth, the Nazis seemed unwilling to legalize the actual murder.

And while there was fear of disclosure lest the world condemn their regime, and deceitfulness was practiced at all levels to hide what they were doing, the Nazis left ample incriminating evidence in a precise paper trail of transit orders and death lists, and in the physical form of gas chambers and crematoria.

© Project Gideon Company, 2023

A sizeable slave labor force, considered essential to the war effort, was employed both for Nazi projects and the industrial complex/factory jobs. Yet, the laborers were literally starved and worked to death, particularly in the concentration camps. There does not appear to be a rational reason for mistreating the workers when productivity could have been increased and attrition decreased (generally desired outcomes) providing adequate food and better work conditions.

The most profound paradox is that a society with a rich heritage of cultural and intellectual achievements could turn itself into a totalitarian regime that perpetrated such unthinkable evil.

Not enough can be written about the Holocaust. It defies description. Language is not adequate to convey the degree of horror, brutality, suffering. Primo Levy, a concentration camp survivor, said, "If the Lagers [German word for camps] had lasted longer, a new, harsh language would have been born; and only this language could express what it means to toil the whole day in the wind, with the temperatures below freezing, wearing only a shirt, underpants, cloth jacket and trousers, and in one's body nothing but weakness, hunger, and knowledge of the end drawing nearer."

The consequences of the Holocaust are lasting. What the Nazis did is a crime against Jews. How they did it is a crime against humanity. Why they did it is inexplicable.

A totalitarian regime wreaked havoc on mankind.

© Project Gideon Company, 2023

I.2 The Role of Psychiatry in the Holocaust

Version 1.0.2

In 2010, Schneider, then president of the DGPPN*, formally asked the victims of the Nazi era and their families for "forgiveness for the pain and injustice [they] suffered in the name of German psychiatry and at the hands of German psychiatrists under National Socialism, and for the silence, trivialization, and denial that for far too long characterized psychiatry in post-war Germany."

German Association for Psychiatry, Psychotherapy and Psychosomatics

Jack Gostl
jgostl@gostl.net

Preface

At Project Gideon we believe that despite the best efforts of researchers and the voluminous documentation available, the core issues of the Holocaust have yet to be addressed. The sheer amount of available detail draws one into studying the trees while missing the forest.

Project Gideon was *NOT* initiated to contradict or challenge the existing research, but rather to probe to a depth that has not yet been explored. Our reasons are simple:

- The souls of six million dead Jews (and many others) deserve to have a better understanding of what transpired
- We believe that it is always better to know than not to know
- To paraphrase Santayana, if we do not learn from this experience, we could repeat it
- The underlying causes of the Holocaust continue to exist, even in the United States, and must be recognized.

It is to this end that this article was written

Contents

1 Introduction 37
    1.1 Prior Research 37
    1.2 Overview 37
2 It is Difficult to Make Sense of the Holocaust 38
    2.1 Key Dates 38
    2.2 Anti-Semitism in Germany 39
3 Evolution Versus Eugenics 39
    3.1 Explanations and Definitions 39
    3.2 The Eugenics Movement 40
    3.3 The Personalities 42
        • Adolf Hitler 42
        • Madison Grant 42
        • Enrich Rüdin 42
4 Euthanasia Centers 43
5 The Schutzstaffel (The SS) 45
6 Propaganda 47
7 Tiergartenstrasse 4 – Aktion T4 49
8 It is Difficult to Make Sense of the Holocaust (Redux) 50
9 Eugenics 50
    9.1 Eugenics and the Holocaust 50
    9.2 Eugenics Today 51
10 Why Have We Not Heard More About This? 52
Appendix – A - Definitions 54
Appendix B – Righteous Among Nations 55
Appendix C – Unsung Heroes 56
    • Drs. Eugeniusz Lazowski and Stanislaw Matulewicz 56
    • Tadeusz Pankiewicz 56
    • Irena Sendler 56

Table of Figures

Figure 1- Key Dates 38
Figure 2 - Map of Euthanasia Centers 43
Figure 3 - Gas Chamber and Mass Graves at Hadamar Facility 44
Figure 4 - Psychiatric Killings in Euthanasia Centers 45
Figure 5 – Percentage of SS Members With PhDs 45
Figure 6 - SS Membership 46
Figure 7 - Publicly Posted Anti-Semitic Propaganda 47
Figure 8 - Killing Film Introduction 48
Figure 9- Films comparing Jews to sewer rats 48
Figure 10 - Poster Blaming Jews for a Typhus Epidemic 48
Figure 11 - Forced Sterilizations 52
Figure 12 - Righteous Among Nations 55
Figure 13 - The Law for Prevention of Genetically Diseased Offspring 57

Change Control

Initial Release	17 Aug 2022
Eliminate Mass Killings graphic and adjust text	18 Aug 2022
Correct reason for outcry regarding euthanasia in T4 project	22 Aug 2022
Miscellaneous spelling and grammar corrections	22 Aug 2022
Add material on post WW2 eugenics	30-Aug 2022
Add material on Martin Grant	22-Sep 2022
Add comments on prior research	23-Sep-2022
Add second chart on SS membership	24-Sep-2022
Add appendix of definitions	30-Sep-2022
Add more on propaganda and "killing films"	02-Oct-2022
Updates to Chapter 110	03-Oct-2022
Add Appendices B and C	03-Oct-2022
Replace Map in Figure 4 and other miscellaneous changes	15-Oct-2022

1 Introduction

1.1 Prior Research

There is a lot of "new" material presented in this article, only it is not "new". It has always been there; it was just necessary to look for it. After almost eight decades of research much of this has still not surfaced. There are some reasons given for this in section 10, but the basic fact remains that because of the unique nature of the Holocaust there is so much information available that it is hard to track. In writing this article I focused on psychiatry, but even then, each time I turned up a fact, it led to a dozen more facts and each of those led to more. Even today, on a regular basis, more paperwork, more archives *even more archaeological evidence emerges.*

I do not wish to fault the hard-working independent researchers who have worked on these matters, and I am especially grateful to the workers at Yad Vashem for their efforts in keeping the memories alive. The events that occurred in the Holocaust were so sweeping and horrific that efforts *must be doubled* lest they become urban legends.

1.2 Overview

This is a discussion of the psychiatric establishment, specifically the German psychiatric establishment, of the 1900-1940s, and the impact it had on the Holocaust. This is not intended to give the psychiatric establishment in general a black eye since the psychiatric establishment helps many people. Rather it is about a rogue group of German physicians who became obsessed with "racial hygiene" and then guided a dictator with similar views down the path of "genetic cleansing".

The Holocaust was a unique event in human history. It was about more than just numbers and the killing of European Jews. Nevertheless, the numbers are important because they give weight to the crimes committed. The Holocaust was a unique event in human history. Most important, when the Holocaust is viewed as just the death of six million Jews, it doesn't make any sense.

Still, numbers, particularly a number like "six million" deserves some attention. It is difficult for a healthy, sane mind, to fully grasp that number. Most significantly, the perception is that these deaths took place over many years, when in fact, the mass killings began in December 1941 and ended in May 1945, or, in other words 42 months. Let's try to bring those numbers down to terms that a healthy mind can grasp.

> Six million deaths in 42 months comes out to over 140,000 deaths *per month*. There are cities smaller than that. Further, this is roughly *4,700 deaths per day*. That is an entire city block in a densely populated area *each day*.

This document tries to show how the German psychiatric establishment encouraged and abetted these deaths. The psychiatric establishment developed techniques for managing victims and performing the killings. This dark corner of the profession further provided the science to justify these mass murders.

> Note: Many of the references in this document came from the Wikipedia. The Wikipedia was used as a convenient summary, and any facts presented were further sourced in other media e.g., Lancet, United States Holocaust Memorial Museum, American Journal of Psychiatry, etc.

2 It is Difficult to Make Sense of the Holocaust
2.1 Key Dates

From a humanistic point of view, it can be said that killings of this magnitude make no sense, but this document approaches these deaths from a practical perspective. The events between 1933 and 1945 demonstrate a series of actions that cannot be solely attributed to the actions of a single anti-Semite magnified by control of one of the largest military machines that ever existed. Let us start by considering the timeline of these events. Figure 1 below summarizes the events.

January 30, 1933*	Hitler becomes Chancellor and effectively assumes total power in Germany.
September 15th 1935	The Nuremburg Race Laws are enacted, effectively totally disenfranchising all Jews in Germany. Considered to be the official start date of the Holocaust.
November 8, 1938*	Kristallnacht (Night of Broken Glass)
January 30th, 1939*	In a speech in the Reichstag, Hitler effectively makes it a capital crime, punishable by death, to be a Jew.
September 1, 1939*	World War 2 starts with the invasion of Poland.
December 7, 1941	Japanese attack on Pearl Harbor.
December 8, 1941*	Chemlo, the first "killing" camp officially opens.
December 8, 1941	The United States declares war on Japan
December 11, 1941	Because of their alliance with Japan, Germany declares war on the United States.
May 7, 1945	Germany surrenders.
May 9, 1945	Allies close the last concentration camp in Stutthof Poland.
August 6th, 1945	Atomic bomb dropped on Hiroshima.
August 9th, 1945	Atomic bomb dropped on Nagasaki
September 2, 1945	Japan surrenders.

Figure 1- Key Dates

Note the dates marked with an asterisk (*), these are of special interest for our purposes and will be subsequently discussed.

The data in this document comes from various sources so it is difficult to construct a linear discussion of this topic, instead, we will cover a number of related topics and then tie things together at the end.

2.2 Anti-Semitism in Germany

Let's look at some key dates.

- In 1933, Germany was one of the best places in Europe to be a Jew. Certainly, there was anti-Semitism, but there was also anti-Semitism in Italy, Austria, Russia and even the UK. I like to think of this as "run of the mill" anti-Semitism.
- In 1935, Jews were totally disenfranchised. Two years *since Hitler came to power*.
- In 1939, being Jewish was a death sentence. Six years in total *since Hitler came to power*.

What we are trying to understand is what happened to cause such a paradigmatic change in so short a period. There was a lot going on in Germany in that timeframe.

- German infrastructure was being rebuilt
- An army was being raised and trained
- German industry was being moved onto a war footing

And still there was enough time to move from "run of the mill" anti-Semitism to the intense, focused anti-Semitism of the Holocaust. While the Nazis were fighting a war on three fronts, Europe, Africa, and Russia, they invested so much time, manpower and resources into the Holocaust that it virtually constituted a fourth front.

3 Evolution Versus Eugenics
3.1 Explanations and Definitions

The worldwide eugenics movements were a key factor driving the change. Before moving forward, it is necessary to be clear on the difference between evolution and eugenics. There are similarities but certain critical differences.

- Evolution – Changes occurring within a species due to environmental changes. The environmental changes could be the result of climate change or introduction of competitive species.[1]
- Eugenics - The study of how to arrange reproduction within a human population to increase the occurrence of heritable characteristics regarded as desirable. Developed largely by Sir Francis Galton as a method of improving the human race, eugenics was increasingly discredited as unscientific and racially biased during the 20th century.[2]

Eugenics has a colorful and somewhat benign history in science fiction, including "Methuselah's Children" by Robert Heinlein, "Ringworld", by Larry Niven, and of course "The Wrath of Kahn" by Gene Rodenberry. Unfortunately, eugenics has a somewhat darker side, most notably involuntary sterilization,

---

[1] This is my definition slightly modified to suit the purposes of this analysis. I believe it to be accurate.
[2] Google's English Dictionary as provided by Oxford Languages.

and outright euthanasia. [Author's note: I have not included an official definition of euthanasia because most "official" definitions stem from kindness and bore scant resemblance to what happened in the Holocaust.] During the holocaust, eugenics took a truly awful turn into "racial hygiene".

3.2 The Eugenics Movement

The eugenics movement started long before the Holocaust and continued long after. The eugenics movement in Germany, and during the Holocaust took a particularly dark, outright proactive, turn. [Author's note: I doubt if there were any "light" turns in this movement.]

In any discussion of eugenics, the terms unfit and undesirable constantly appear. Upon examination, these appear to be political rather than scientific definitions, which of course means that the definitions keep changing. It can be said that the Pharaohs practiced eugenics in Exodus by drowning Jewish infants. The Chinese practiced eugenics by killing (or more recently aborting) female children. More recently, in the 20th century, eugenics came to mean sterilization.

> **Eugenics** is the scientifically erroneous and immoral theory of "racial improvement" and "planned breeding," which gained popularity during the early 20th century. Eugenicists worldwide believed that they could perfect human beings and eliminate so-called social ills through genetics and heredity. They believed the use of methods such as involuntary sterilization, segregation and social exclusion would rid society of individuals deemed by them to be unfit.[3]

The Nazis of course carried this to extremes and performed outright killings.[4]

It should be noted that the United States was not immune to the siren call of eugenics. There was a strong movement in the early part of the twentieth century resulting in the involuntary sterilization of tens of thousands of women. Shockingly, the atrocities of the Holocaust did not end these sterilizations.

> In the 1960s and 1970s, the Indian Health Service (IHS) and its collaborating physicians sustained a practice of performing sterilizations on Native American women, in many cases without the informed consent of their patients.

Unfortunately, this still goes on today.

> In 2013, it was reported that 148 female prisoners in two California prisons were sterilized between 2006 and 2010 in a supposedly voluntary program, but it was determined that the prisoners did not give consent to the procedures.[5] In September 2014, California enacted Bill SB1135 that bans sterilization in correctional facilities, unless the procedure is required to save an inmate's life.[6]

---

[3] National Human Genome Institute – Fact Sheet

[4] I chose to avoid the argument as to whether this was "murder" or "killing". Under Nazi German laws, these deaths were based on existing legal structures, hence they were "killings", not murder. This distinction is covered in numerous Torah commentaries.

[5] "Sterilization Abuse in State Prisons" by Alex Stern

[6] SBA 1135 CA Gov

Yet these actions in the US are thoroughly overshadowed by involuntary sterilizations in other parts of the world as is noted Figure 11 on page 52.

So, the idea is not new. There is considerable written material on the topic, but it is best to move forward with the discussion of the involvement of the German psychiatric establishment in the Holocaust.

3.3 The Personalities

There are three key names that should be mentioned in connection with this topic. In brief.

- Adolf Hitler – Of course this topic cannot be discussed without some mention of Adolf Hitler. Hitler dropped out of school at 15. As often happens in these cases, he was always seeking validation of his ideas. That, combined with a natural anti-Semitism and connecting with the right people at the right time, led to the Holocaust.

- Madison Grant – An American lawyer, anthropologist, writer, and zoologist known primarily for his work as a eugenicist and conservationist, an advocate of scientific racism, and as one of the leading thinkers and activists of the Progressive Era.

  Grant's work was embraced by proponents of the National Socialist movement in Germany and was the first non-German book ordered to be reprinted by the Nazis when they took power. Adolf Hitler wrote to Grant, "The book is my Bible."

  At the postwar Nuremberg Trials, three pages of excerpts from Grant's *Passing of the Great Race* were introduced into evidence by the defense of Karl Brandt, Hitler's personal physician and head of the Nazi euthanasia program, in order to justify the population policies of the Third Reich, or at least indicate that they were not ideologically unique to Nazi Germany

- Enrich Rüdin – This man may be the key to the whole puzzle. Born in 1893, a renowned psychiatrist and a major advocate of the idea that the German race was becoming "polluted"[7]

    At a conference on alcoholism in 1903, he argued for the sterilization of 'incurable alcoholics', but his proposal was roundly defeated. In 1904, he was appointed co-editor in chief of the newly founded Archive for Racial Hygiene and Social Biology, and in 1905 was among the co-founders of the German Society for Racial Hygiene (which soon became international). He published an article of his own in Archives in 1910, in which he argued *that medical care for the mentally ill, alcoholics, epileptics and others was a distortion of natural laws of natural selection, and medicine should help to clean the genetic pool.*

---

[7] Brüne, Martin (1 January 2007). "On human self-domestication, psychiatry, and eugenics". *Philosophy, Ethics, and Humanities in Medicine.* **2** (1): 21. doi:10.1186/1747-5341-2-21. PMC 2082022. PMID 17919321.

Perhaps his personality and views are best summarized by the following quote:

> *In 1942, speaking about 'euthanasia', Rüdin emphasized "the value of eliminating young children of clearly inferior quality".*

This was a psychiatrist and a racist and a strong advocate of euthanasia of "inferiors". He joined the Nazi party in 1937, and for Rüdin and Hitler, it was love at first sight.

Rüdin gave Hitler something he craved, a scientific basis for his beliefs. Hitler gave Rüdin what he needed, funding to implement his ideas. This was the perfect storm. Shortly thereafter "euthanasia centers" (see section 4 below) began to appear throughout Germany.

One could easily nominate Rüdin as "The Father of the Holocaust".

4   Euthanasia Centers

In 1939, with Hitler's financial backing, a series of "euthanasia centers" began to appear.

> *Beginning in the fall of 1939, gassing installations were established at Bernburg, Brandenburg, Grafeneck, Hadamar, Hartheim, and Sonnenstein. Patients were selected by doctors and transferred from clinics to one of these centralized gassing installations and killed.[8]*

These "euthanasia centers" were widespread throughout Germany.

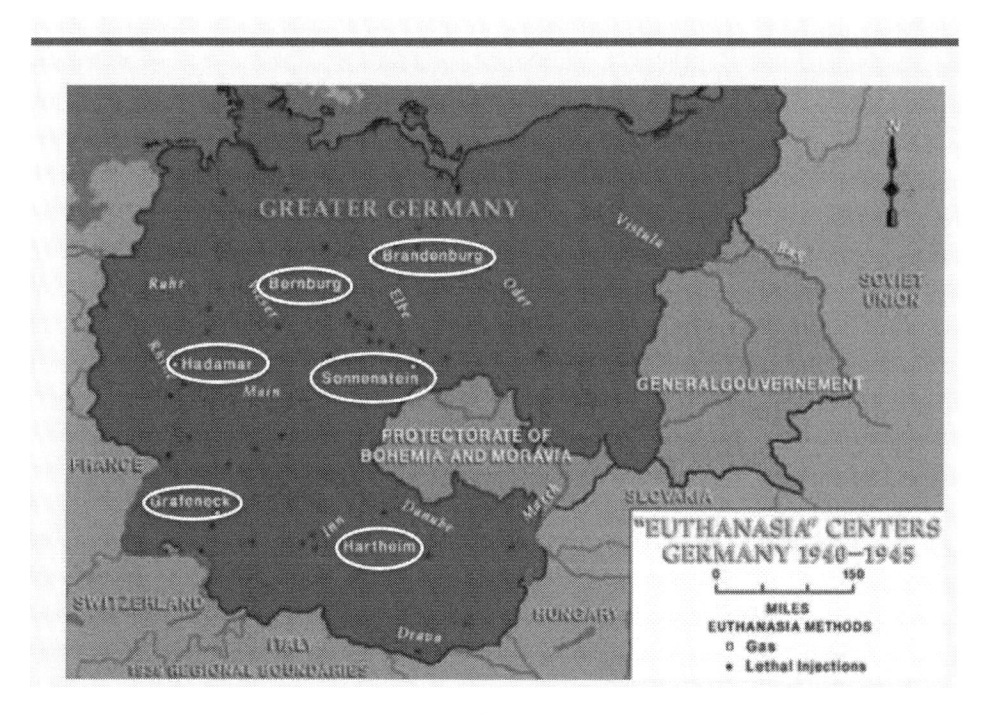

Figure 2 - Map of Euthanasia Centers

---

[8] United States Holocaust Memorial Museum

It was at these centers that the prototype for the mass killings was developed. The "patients" were gassed, and bodies cremated.

The German medical profession was forced to switch to "local" euthanasia via injection. It would be nice to assume that this was due to a sudden burst of philosemitism[9], but more likely it was because the public discovered that many of those killed were lower rung Christian clerics and others who protested government actions.

And so it begins:

> On January 9, [1939] the first "gassing test" using carbon monoxide took place in the Brandenburg sanitarium. Between 18 and 20 people were killed, watched by psychiatrists, physicians, and nurses. In 1941, the psychiatric institution at Hadamar celebrated the cremation of its 10,000th patient where everyone—secretaries, nurses, and psychiatrists—received a bottle of beer for the occasion.

It is important to note that this was almost three years before the first mass killing facility, Chemlo, went into operation. When Chemlo went into operation, the killing became an industry.

> By 1940, six killing centers designated as euthanasia institutions were established at Brandenburg, Grafeneck, Hartheim, Sonnenstein, Bernburg, and Hadamar. The Hadamar Psychiatric Institute near Wiesbaden, Germany, code-named "Facility-E," was refashioned for use as a psychiatry euthanasia facility in November 1940. From mid-January 1941 under Dr. Ernst Baumhard's direction, with a staff of approximately 100, busloads of patients arrived daily at the killing operation. The patients were offloaded, weighed, photographed, and led to the gas chamber disguised as a shower room in the cellar. At least 10,000 mentally ill adults were gassed and cremated at Hadamar in the first 9 months of 1941. In August 1942, after a short break, the facility again functioned as a euthanasia center, using lethal medication doses or starvation. After removal of various organs for medical research, the bodies were buried in mass graves located on the hospital grounds. The killing center remained operational until its liberation by American troops on March 26, 1945.[10]

Figure 3 - Gas Chamber and Mass Graves at Hadamar Facility

---

[9] A notable interest in, respect for, and appreciation of the Jewish people.
[10] The American Journal of Psychiatry, January 2006

The Holocaust Wars
The Role of Psychiatry

The following table shows the number of killings between 1939 and 1941.

T4 Center	Operation timetable	Number of victims
T4 Center	From	Total
Grafeneck	20 January 1940	9,839
Brandenburg	8 February 1940	9,772
Bernburg	21 November 1940	8,601
Hartheim	6 May 1940	18,269
Sonnenstein	June 1940	13,720
Hadamar	January 1941	10,072
Total		70,273

Figure 4 - Psychiatric Killings in Euthanasia Centers

5   The Schutzstaffel (The SS)

One of the big surprises in this research, and one of the key pieces in the puzzle involved the Schutzstaffel, the SS. The SS was the organization most responsible for the genocidal murder of an estimated 5.5 to 6 million Jews and millions of other victims during the Holocaust.[11] It is popular belief that the SS was constituted of a group of uneducated thugs. Thugs perhaps, but not uneducated.

- In 1933, when Hitler took power, 40% of the psychiatrists in Germany were members of the SS.[12]
- The level of education in the SS was far superior to that of the German public in general.

Percentage of SS With PhDs

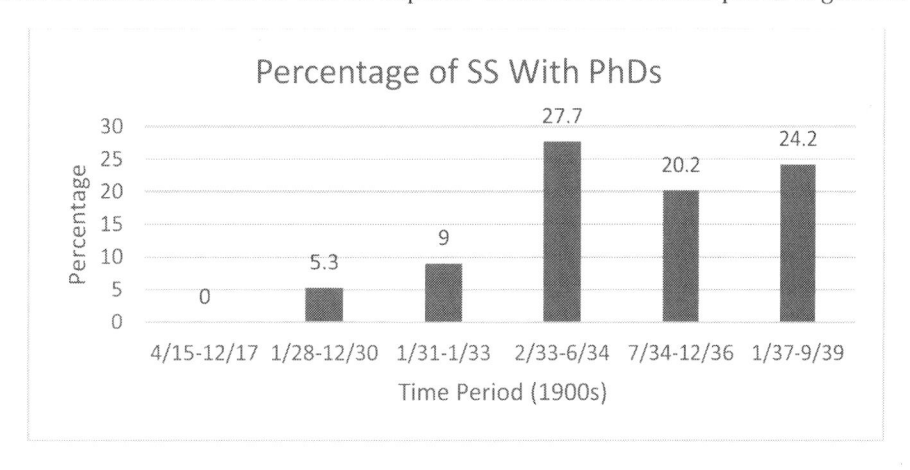

Time Period (1900s)	Percentage
4/15-12/17	0
1/28-12/30	5.3
1/31-1/33	9
2/33-6/34	27.7
7/34-12/36	20.2
1/37-9/39	24.2

Figure 5 – Percentage of SS Members With PhDs[13]

---

[11] Buchenwald, Dachau, Flossenbürg, Mauthausen, Ravensbrück, and Sachsenhausen.[100]
Not to be confused with *SS-Sonderkommandos*, ad hoc SS units that used the same name.
Evans 2008, p. 318

[12] Attribution needed.

[13] **AN ANALYSIS OF THE AGE AND EDUCATION OF THE SS FÜHRERKORPS 1925 – 1939**, Gunnar C. Boehnert

© Project Gideon Company, 2023

The Holocaust Wars
The Role of Psychiatry

While it is true that the SS troops that did the "grunt" work (mostly NCOs), the actual operation of the killing camps, were *relatively* poorly educated, the SS was run by the intellectual elite of Germany.

It should not be missed that in the period immediately following Hitler's ascension to power, the education level in the SS nearly tripled. These numbers are even more surprising considering the rapid grown of SS membership in the same period.

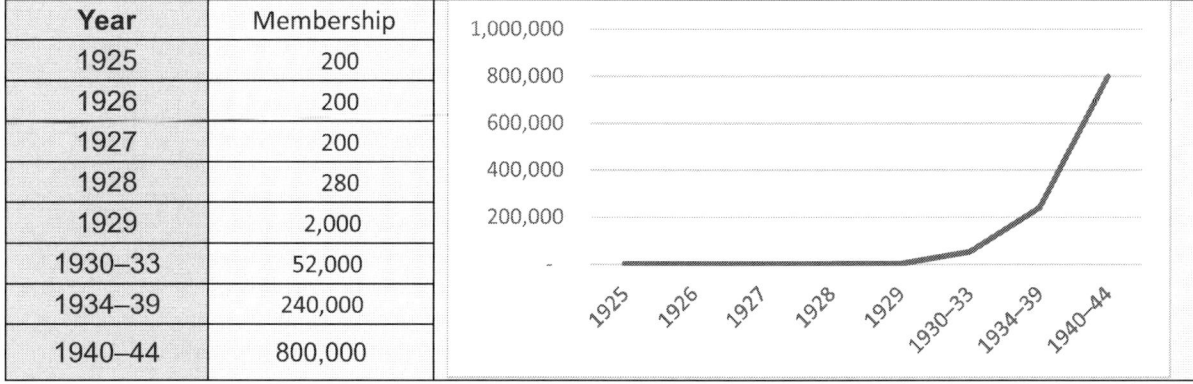

Year	Membership
1925	200
1926	200
1927	200
1928	280
1929	2,000
1930–33	52,000
1934–39	240,000
1940–44	800,000

Figure 6 - SS Membership[14]

Combining these two sets of figures, we see that:

- In 1933 we have approximately 5,000 PhDs in the SS
- In 1940 we have approximately 60,000 PhDs in the SS
- By the end of the war, we have close to *a quarter million* PhDs in the SS.

So, while it is attractive to think of the SS as a bunch of ignorant goons, instead we find a highly educated, well trained membership with the mission of enforcing the "ethnic hygiene" rules.

---

[14] Various sources

© Project Gideon Company, 2023

6 Propaganda

Once again, I come back to the statements that the change from "run of the mill anti-Semitism" to a genocide, accepted by an educated populace, in under six years seems inconsistent. The answer lies in an intense propaganda campaign, likely run by trained psychiatric professionals.

A discussion of the propaganda campaign can be found in an article published by the United States Holocaust Memorial Museum.

> https://encyclopedia.ushmm.org/content/en/article/nazi-propaganda

The Nazis used skilled propagandists to use all available means of the time, movies, newspapers, and posters, to spread the message:

- The Jews were evil
- The Jews were diluting Aryan blood
- The Jews were Communists, hence linked to the Russian enemy

Figure 7, Figure 8, Figure 9, and Figure 10 below. are examples of the constant barrage of anti-Semitic propaganda.

Outdoor display of the antisemitic newspaper Der Stürmer

A German couple reads an outdoor display of the antisemitic newspaper *Der Stürmer* (The Attacker). Germany, 1935.

- *Nederlands Institute voor Oorlogsdocumentatie*

Figure 7 - Publicly Posted Anti-Semitic Propaganda

Using the full array of available technology, the Nazis produced a series of movies called Killing Films. These were mandatory viewing and were presented in all theaters.

Title: A Film Contribution On the Problem of World Jewry

Figure 8 - Killing Film Introduction

A common theme was to compare Jews to teeming packs of disease infested sewer rats.

Verbiage with this segment talks about how sewer rats, bringing diseases such as:
- Plague
- Leprosy
- Typhus
- Cholera
- Dysentery

Figure 9- Films comparing Jews to sewer rats

This is a particularly ugly poster blaming the Jews for a local typhus epidemic. It turns out that the Germans were particularly fearful of typhus.

Ironically, the epidemic described in this poster was a false one, perpetrated to protect the local Jewish population. (See Appendix C – Unsung Heroes.)

Figure 10 - Poster Blaming Jews for a Typhus Epidemic

One can well imagine the psychic impact on the German public of a constant bombardment of this type of material.

7 Tiergartenstrasse 4 – Aktion T4

No discussion of the Holocaust is complete without a discussion of Aktion T4. Many consider Aktion T4 to be the dress rehearsal for the Holocaust.

> *The [T4] Euthanasia Program represented in many ways a rehearsal for Nazi Germany's subsequent genocidal policies. The Nazi leadership extended the ideological justification conceived by medical perpetrators for the destruction of the "unfit" to other categories of perceived biological enemies, most notably to Jews and* **Roma** *(Gypsies).*
>
> *Planners of the "**Final Solution**" later borrowed the gas chamber and accompanying crematoria, specifically designed for the T4 campaign, to murder Jews in German-occupied Europe. T4 personnel who had shown themselves reliable in this first mass murder program figured prominently among the German staff stationed at the* **Operation Reinhard killing centers of Belzec, Sobibor, and Treblinka.**

The description of the operation of Aktion T4 bears an uncomfortable resemblance to an Orwellian novel.[15]

> *Beginning in October 1939, public health authorities began to encourage parents of children with disabilities to admit their young children to one of a number of specially designated pediatric clinics throughout Germany and Austria. In reality, the clinics were children's killing wards. There, specially recruited medical staff, murdered their young charges by lethal overdoses of medication or by starvation.*

There is not much more to say about this. It was methodical, cold blooded and efficient, and, under guidance of medical professions It grew into the Holocaust.

---

[15] Material from the United States Memorial Holocaust Museum

8 It is Difficult to Make Sense of the Holocaust (Redux)

The Holocaust would seem to make no sense because:

- It came about so quickly
- The resources invested in it were tantamount to a *fourth* front in the war.[16]
- The propaganda campaign was intense and of professional quality
- One man's hatred of Jews couldn't explain all the above

But look deeper:

- When you look to the past, prior to 1933, to the beginning of eugenics in the 19th century
- When you look at the combination of Hitler and Rüdin
- When you see the euthanasia centers already operating in 1939-1941 (see section 4, page 43)
- When you see the constant involvement of the psychiatric establishment

Then a pattern emerges in which the Holocaust is clearly the end product of an intense eugenics "experiment" orchestrated and run by the German psychiatric establishment.

9 Eugenics

9.1 Eugenics and the Holocaust

A straight line can be drawn from the creation of the "science" of eugenics to the Holocaust.

> *The term* eugenics *was coined in 1883 by British explorer and natural scientist Francis Galton, who, influenced by Charles Darwin's theory of natural selection, advocated a system that would allow "the more suitable races or strains of blood a better chance of prevailing speedily over the less suitable."*[17]

Yet eugenics alone cannot explain what happened in 1933-1945. There were several other elements involved.

- An underlying prejudice (anti-Semitism)
- An established scientific community (the psychiatric establishment) lending credibility to eugenics
- A totalitarian state that
    - Provided personnel and funding on a nation state level
    - Created a huge propaganda campaign inflaming the underlying prejudice
    - A legal structure that lent moral credence the eugenics recommendations

---

[16] Europe, Africa, and Russia representing the three fronts.
[17] Online Britannica. Philip K. Wilson. https://www.britannica.com/science/eugenics-genetics

- Allowed implementation of the most drastic eugenics recommendations

Remove any one of these elements, and you do not have the Holocaust. The Holocaust was truly a unique event in human history. A true crime against humanity. That is not to say that it could not occur again, but those elements, or their equivalent, would be a necessary condition.

There are lessons to be drawn from this, all of which I will not attempt to enumerate, but we can start with:

- Relying on "science" alone is not sufficient because "science" is at the mercy of "scientists". Scientists are people and people can be wrong or can have personal agendas.
- Oddly, from these atrocities we can see an underlying good in people.
  - The need to "convince" the German people through a combination of laws and propaganda.
  - The post World War 2 reaction of [most] of the world
  - The efforts of the German government in subsequent years to "clear its name"
  - In Poland, there were many heroic actions. (Appendix C – Unsung Heroes, provides more information on some of these people.)
    - Many Catholic clergy as well as Jews were killed
    - In an amazing display of ingenuity and courage, Drs. Eugene Lazowski and Dr. Stanislaw Matulewicz, Polish physicians, risked their lives to provide medical treatment and protection for Polish Jews. They saved some 8,000 Jews (See Appendix C)
    - Social worker Irena Sendler, saved over 2,500 Jewish children[18]
  - Read **Appendix C – Unsung Heroes**, for more information on the conspicuous bravery displayed by many

So, there is a lesson here, one with many parts, but a complicated one.

9.2 Eugenics Today

It would be nice to say that the lessons of 1933-1945 were the end of the "science" of eugenics. That would be nice, but naïve. Eugenics outlasted World War 2 and is still alive and well today, both around the world and in the United States. Such was the power of this unique event, the Holocaust. Eugenics has a seductive appeal, after all, who could object to improving humanity. Unfortunately, eugenics proposes *forced* changes, frequently enforced on the powerless.

> *Whereas eugenic sterilization programs before World War II were mostly conducted on prisoners or patients in mental hospitals, after the war, compulsory sterilizations were targeted at poor people and minorities.[19] As a result of these new sterilization initiatives, though most scholars agree that there were over 64,000 known cases of eugenic*

---

[18] https://www.neh.gov/article/irena-sendler-and-girls-kansas
https://www.coffeeordie.com/irena-sendler

[19] Begos, Kevin (18 May 2011). "The American eugenics movement after World War II (part 1 of 3)". *INDY Week*.

> sterilization in the U.S. by 1963, no one knows for certain how many compulsory sterilizations occurred between the late 1960s to 1970s, though it is estimated that at least 80,000 may have been conducted. A large number of those who were targets of coerced sterilizations in the latter half of the century were African American, Hispanic, and Native American women.

As disturbing as these numbers are, they pale compared to what happened in Europe and the rest of the world.

- Germany – Prior to the war 600,000
- Germany – During the war 400,000
- Denmark 60,000
- Sweden .... 21,000[20]
- China – One child policy .... Unknown

Figure 11 - Forced Sterilizations

There has been a tremendous amount written on this subject, and it is beyond the scope of this document to address all of it. This document has attempted to focus on the role of the psychiatric establishment in the Holocaust. Nevertheless, the echoes of the events of 1935-1945 are still with us today.

10 Why Have We Not Heard More About This?

There is a great deal of talk about how the United States could have done more to help the Jews of Europe. These stories obscure the fact that the United States and Denmark were *the only countries that actually did anything to help the European Jews*. There is a world of difference between "doing nothing" and "not doing enough". We can argue endlessly about "doing enough" but we can't overlook the actions taken and the moral courage required to take those actions.

After the end of World War 2, as the Nuremberg trials began, a large number of psychiatrists were due to stand trial. The American Psychiatric Association feared that because of the actions of these psychiatrists the profession would carry a permanent black mark, so pressure was applied to minimize the number of psychiatric defendants.

The involvement of Ernst Rüdin was thoroughly whitewashed. Three types of accounts have been identified:

- Those who write about German psychiatric genetics in the Nazi period, but either fail to mention Rüdin at all, or cast him in a favorable light

---

[20] Does not include some 6,000 "voluntary" (but coerced) sterilizations.

- Those who acknowledge that Rüdin helped promote eugenic sterilization and/or may have worked with the Nazis, but generally paint a positive picture of Rüdin's research and fail to mention his participation in the "euthanasia" killing program
- Those who have written that Rüdin committed and supported unspeakable atrocities."

After the war, the German Medical Association blamed Nazi atrocities on a small group of 350 criminal doctors.[21] It was not until the 21st century that the truth started to appear.

And let us never forget how massive these events were and it is easy to miss details, even significant details.

The are some embarrassing facts that produce tremendous incentives to keep this material downplayed.

- The involvement of Madison Grant is something most of us would rather forget.
- There was a need to allow Germany to "cleanse" itself and rejoin the world community. (Perhaps a lesson learned from the treaties that ended World War 1?)
- As of January 2022, in the United States[22]:
    - 31 states plus Washington, D.C., have laws explicitly allowing the forced sterilization of disabled people, most recently passed in 2019 in Iowa and Nevada
    - 17 states allow forced sterilizations on disabled children
    - Only three states explicitly prohibit it on disabled children
    - 11 states and Washington, D.C., do not have specific language on minors
- In the rest of the world, the eugenics and sterilization programs are still active

So, the eugenics movement continues to exist, another painful legacy of the Holocaust.

Personally, I have always felt that it is a mistake to downplay this material. If you don't shine a bright light on this type of evil, it retreats underground and grow unchecked. The perception is that the Holocaust was the work of a brilliant but sociopathic Bavarian house painter. That is wrong, or at least incomplete. The truth is much more complicated. This document barely scratches the surface.

Why was this document prepared?

- The souls of six million dead Jews (and many others) deserve to have the truth known
- I have always felt that it is better to know than not to know
- To paraphrase Santayana, if we don't learn from this, we could repeat it
- The underlying causes continue to live in the world and in the United States.

---

[21] Kolb, Stephan; Weindling, Paul; Roelcke, Volker; Seithe, Horst (2012). *"Apologising for Nazi medicine: A constructive starting point"*. *The Lancet*. **380** (9843): 722–723. *doi:10.1016/S0140-6736(12)61396-8*. PMC 4365922. PMID 22928190.
[22] Rewire News Group, JAN 25, 2022, 12:30PM, ANAGHA SRIKANTH

Appendix – A- Definitions

Eugenics

The study of how to arrange reproduction within a human population to increase the occurrence of heritable characteristics regarded as desirable.
Oxford Languages

Euthanasia

An easy or painless death, or the intentional ending of the life of a person suffering from an incurable or painful disease at his or her request. Also called mercy killing.
NCI Dictionary of Cancer Terms

Evolution

The gradual development of something, especially from a simple to a more complex form.
Oxford Languages

Holocaust

Destruction or slaughter on a mass scale, especially caused by fire or nuclear war.
Oxford Languages

Murder

To kill (someone) <u>*unlawfully*</u> and with premeditation. [Author's emphasis]
Oxford Languages

Psychiatry

The branch of medicine focused on the diagnosis, treatment and prevention of mental, emotional and behavioral disorders.
American Psychiatric Association

SS – *Schutzstaffel*

Protection Squadrons- A virtual state within a state in Nazi Germany, staffed by men who perceived themselves as the "racial elite" of Nazi future.
Holocaust Encyclopedia

Appendix B – Righteous Among Nations

An honorific used by the State of Israel to describe non-Jews who risked their lives during the Holocaust to save Jews from extermination by the Nazis for altruistic reasons. As of 1 January 2021, the award has been made to 27,921 people. This Yad Vashem highlights that the table is not representative of the effort or proportion of Jews saved per country, and notes that these numbers "are not necessarily an indication of the actual number of rescuers in each country but reflect the cases that were made available to Yad Vashem.

Below is a partial list.

Country	Number of awards	Notable recipients
Poland	7,177	Jan Karski, Maria Kotarba, Irena Sendler, Irena Adamowicz
Netherlands	5,910	Frits Philips, Jan Zwartendijk
France	4,150	Anne Beaumanoir, Jeanne Brousse
Ukraine	2,673	Klymentiy Sheptytsky
Belgium	1,774	Queen Elisabeth of Belgium
Lithuania	918	Ona Šimaitė
Hungary	876	Endre Szervánszky, Sára Salkaházi
Italy	744	Giorgio Perlasca, Gino Bartali, Giuseppe Girotti, Odoardo Focherini
Belarus	676	
Germany	641	Oskar Schindler, Wilm Hosenfeld, Hans von Dohnanyi, Bernhard Lichtenberg

Figure 12 - Righteous Among Nations

The Holocaust Wars
The Role of Psychiatry

Appendix C – Unsung Heroes
Just a few of the notable, courageous, Polish citizens who risked their lives to save Jews.

- Drs. Eugeniusz Lazowski and Stanislaw Matulewicz - In Rozwadow, Drs. Lazowski and Matulewicz (left) are credited with saving approximately 8,000 Jews by putting their medical knowledge to use. Having injected the town's Jews with a benign form of typhus he then informed the Nazis that an epidemic was at large. Terrified that it would spread, the Nazis quarantined the town and left it to its own devices. Known as 'the Polish Schindlers,' the two of them saved 12 ghetto communities in this crafty manner. "I was not able to fight with a gun or a sword," Lazowski said. "But I was able to find a way to scare the Germans."

- Tadeusz Pankiewicz - Within the Kraków Ghetto there were four prewar pharmacies owned by non-Jews. Tadeusz Pankiewicz was the only proprietor to decline the German offer of relocating to the gentile (non-Jewish) side of the city. He was given permission to continue operating his establishment as the only pharmacy in the Ghetto.

  The often-scarce medications and pharmaceutical products supplied to the ghetto's residents, often free of charge, substantially improved their quality of life. In effect, apart from health care considerations, they contributed to survival itself. In his published testimonies, Praniewicz makes particular mention of hair dyes used by those disguising their identities and tranquilizers given to fretful children required to keep silent during Gestapo raids.

- Irena Sendler - Another doctor, **Irena Sendler**, is credited with rescuing over 2,500 Jews from the Warsaw ghetto. Head of the children's section of Zegota – a secret organization that was a 'Council to Aid Jews'. Her actions aroused the attention of the Gestapo, and in 1943 she was arrested, tortured, and sentenced to death. A bribe saved her life, but nonetheless she was left unconscious in a forest, with both her arms and legs broken.

© Project Gideon Company, 2023

11 Appendix D – Germany's "Sterilization Law"

Figure 13 - The Law for Prevention of Genetically Diseased Offspring

The Law for the Prevention of Genetically Diseased Offspring "Sterilization Law" was a statute in Nazi Germany enacted on July 14, 1933.

It created "Genetic Health Courts", consisting of a judge, a medical officer, and medical practitioner, which "shall decide at its own discretion after considering the results of the whole proceedings and the evidence tendered". The sterilization was to be carried out, with the law specifying that "the use of force is permissible". The law also required that people seeking voluntary sterilizations also go through the courts.

In the first year of the law's operation, 1934, 84,600 cases were brought to Genetic Health Courts, with 62,400 forced sterilizations. In 1935, there were 88,100 trials and 71,700 sterilizations.[5] By the end of the Nazi regime, over 200 "Genetic Health Courts" were created, and under their rulings over 400,000 people were sterilized against their will.[6]

Along with the law, Adolf Hitler personally decriminalized abortion in case of fetuses having racial or hereditary defects for doctors, while the abortion of healthy "pure" German, "Aryan" unborn remained strictly forbidden.

At the time of its enaction, the German government pointed to the success of sterilization laws elsewhere as evidence of the humaneness and efficacy of such laws. Eugenicists abroad admired the German law for its legal and ideological clarity. American eugenicist Popenoe wrote that "the German law is well drawn and, in form, may be considered better than the sterilization laws of most American states", and trusted in the German government's "conservative, sympathetic, and intelligent administration" of the law, praising the "scientific leadership" of the Nazis.

Below is a list of "defects" from the law. Note that many are psychiatric in nature, and some are quite subjective.

- Congenital Mental Deficiency
- Schizophrenia
- Manic-Depressive Insanity
- Hereditary epilepsy
- Hereditary chorea (Huntington's)
- Hereditary blindness
- Hereditary deafness
- Any severe hereditary deformity
- Severe alcoholism

The Uprisings of the Jews and The Role of Jewish Partisans During the Holocaust

Entire battalions were removed from the front lines to deal with the "partisan problem.

Jack Gostl
jgostl@gostl.net

Preface

This article is about Jewish resistance during the Holocaust. It covers uprisings in the camps, partisan activities and more. It is by no means intended to be an exhaustive study of the topic, rather it is intended to punch a hole in the myth that all Jews meekly walked into gas chambers. The purpose is to reduce victimology associated with Jews and World War 2. And as always, at least in what I write, there is a discussion of "the good guys". The non-Jews who risked their lives to save Jewish lives.

We believe that in all memorials and educational programs the audience must:

- Get a pain and suffering tale so that tears will flow for the tormented dead and for the survivors whose lives were destroyed.
- Hear pain and suffering tales that impact the offspring (already three generations) for whom the tears are not enough and remembering with anger is helpful for numerous reasons.
- Hear tales of the tears and sorrow in which it is imperative to show that mere defiance is heroic in the face of the horrendous crimes of deranged criminals.
- Hear of the actual lethal heroic acts that were delivered by Jews with very meager means but enormous courage.
- Honor the incredible gentiles who received a well-earned "Jewish Medal of Honor" (many thousands of them) in the form of and the recognition of being "Righteous Among Nations" (see page 75).

Contents

1 Introduction 62
2 The SS Schutzstaffel 63
3 The Warsaw Ghetto Uprising 64
4 Jewish Uprisings in the Camps 65
    4.1   The Uprising in Treblinka   65
    4.2   Uprising at Sobibor   66
    4.3   Uprising at Auschwitz-Birkenau 66
5 Partisans 66
    5.1   What is a Partisan   67
    5.2   What Defines Resistance   67
    5.3   Some Key Dates 68
    5.4   Where Did Jewish Partisans Fight   69
    5.5   All Women Partisan Brigades   69
        5.5.1   Introduction 69
        5.5.2   Russia (Vilna) Haika Grosman 70
        5.5.3   Poland Eta Wrobel 70
        5.5.4   Poland: Tosia Altman 71
        5.5.5   Hungary: Hannah Senesh 71
    5.6   Lithuania and Byelorussia   71
6 Non-Resistance Resistance and the "Good Guys" 73
    6.1   Introduction   73
    6.2   Poland: Drs. Eugeniusz Lazowski and Stanislaw Matulewicz   73
    6.3   Poland: Tadeusz Pankiewicz   73
    6.4   Poland: Irena Sendler   73
Appendix A – Jewish of US Medal of Honor Winners 74
Appendix B – Righteous Among Nations 75

Table of Figures

Figure 1 - Percentage of SS Members With PhDs	63
Figure 2 - SS Membership	64
Figure 3 - Polish soldier firing a Błyskawica during the Warsaw Uprising	65
Figure 4 - Filipinka – right; Sidolowka – Left. By Halibutt – CC BY-SA 3.0	65
Figure 5 - Róza Robota, participant in the Auschwitz-Birkenau revolt of October 1944	66
Figure 6 - Map of Jewish Partisan Fighting	69
Figure 7 - Haika Grossman	70
Figure 8 - Eta Wrobel	70
Figure 9 - Tosia Altman	71
Figure 10 - Hannah Szenes	71
Figure 11 - Drs. Lazowski and Matulewicz (left)	73
Figure 12 - Tadeusz Pankiewicz	73
Figure 13 - Righteous Among Nations	75

The Holocaust Wars
They Didn't Go Quietly

1 Introduction

The classic view of the Holocaust includes long lines of Jews timidly walking into the gas chambers. This is far from the truth. The image of the skinny, bespectacled, bearded victim belies the true facts. Whether it was through generations of breeding for intelligence, or perhaps being survivors of years of anti-Semitism, many of the Holocaust victims were intelligent and tough. Tough enough to cause the German war machine considerable grief.

Consider the size and resources of the Schutzstaffel (the SS). The primary mission of the SS was to enforce the racial purity laws. By the end of the war the SS consisted almost a half million people, volunteers that included the intellectual elite of Germany. Normally in an army the ratio of enlisted men to officers is four to one. Because of the high caliber of their membership, there is apocryphal evidence that this is conservative for the SS, so as a paramilitary organization let us consider this the equivalent of a million men. And that was just for "normal" enforcement of the purity laws. Going beyond this, the resistance, the partisans, which tend to be ignored, drained further resources from the Nazi war machine.

By the middle of the war Germany was taking a beating on three fronts, Russia, Europe and Africa. The investment of time and energy in "the Jewish problem" was tantamount to a fourth front. The siphoning of these resources by the Jewish resistance represents a significant contribution to the Allied war effort.

I'm particularly fond of the following quotes from the movie (and true story) "The Great Escape". This first quote is from the words of the commandant of the Prisoner of War camp:

> *In the past four years the Reich has been forced to spend an enormous amount of time, energy, manpower and equipment hunting down escaping prisoner-of-war officers.*

Similarly, the British officer in charge of the escapes said:

> *I'm going to cause such a terrible stink in this... Third Reich of theirs, that thousands of troops that could well be employed at the front will be tied up here looking after us.*

This is precisely what happened when the "meek" Jews showed their determination and strength. All POW escapes were admirable, but were small stuff compared to the effort put into quelling Jewish uprisings and countering Jewish "guerrilla" activities.

2 The SS Schutzstaffel

One of the big surprises in this research, and one of the key pieces in the puzzle involved the Schutzstaffel, the SS.

An obvious question is why discuss the SS in an article about uprisings. The answer is simple, in order to gauge the value of an encounter one must evaluate the quality of one's enemies. The SS had the ultimate responsibility for carrying out the "ethnic cleansing" and the "Final Solution to the Jewish Problem." The popular perception is that they were ignorant, arrogant bullies. In fact while it is true that they were arrogant bullies they were far from ignorant. They were in fact the acme of German intellectuals.

The SS was the organization most responsible for the genocidal murder of an estimated 5.5 to 6 million Jews and millions of other victims during the Holocaust[23]. It is popular belief that the SS was constituted of a group of uneducated thugs. Thugs perhaps, but not uneducated.

- In 1933, when Hitler took power, 40% of the psychiatrists in Germany were members of the SS[24].
- The level of education in the SS was far superior to that of the German public in general.

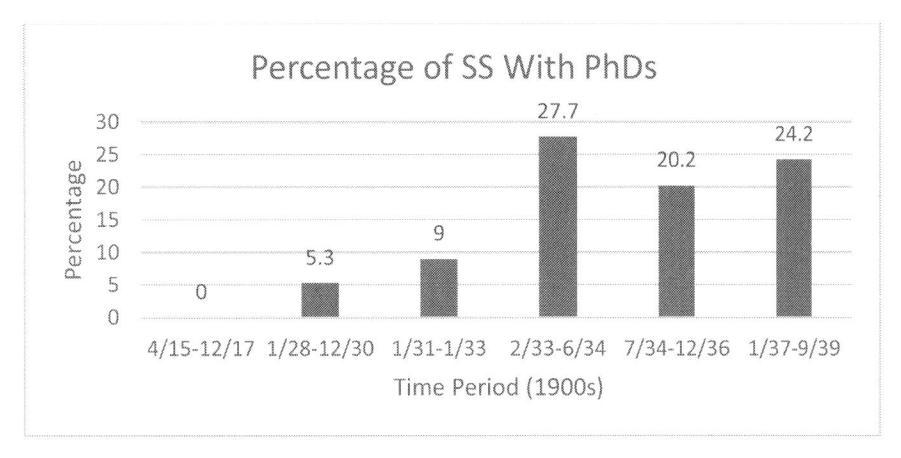

Figure 14 - Percentage of SS Members With PhDs[25]

While it is true that the SS troops that did the "grunt" work, and the actual operation of the killing camps, were mostly NCOs, and were *relatively* poorly educated, the SS was run by the intellectual elite of Germany.

It should not be missed that in the period immediately following Hitler's ascension to power, the education level in the SS nearly tripled. These numbers are even more surprising considering the rapid growth of SS membership in the same period. See Figure 15 below.

---

[23] Buchenwald, Dachau, Flossenbürg, Mauthausen, Ravensbrück, and Sachsenhausen.[100]
Not to be confused with *SS-Sonderkommandos*, ad hoc SS units that used the same name.
Evans 2008, p. 318

[24] Attribution needed.

[25] AN ANALYSIS OF THE AGE AND EDUCATION OF THE SS FÜHRERKORPS 1925 – 1939, Gunnar C. Boehnert

The Holocaust Wars
They Didn't Go Quietly

Year	Membership
1925	200
1926	200
1927	200
1928	280
1929	2,000
1930–33	52,000
1934–39	240,000
1940–44	800,000

Figure 15 - SS Membership[26]

Combining these two sets of figures, we see that:

- In 1933 we have approximately 5,000 PhDs in the SS
- In 1940 we have approximately 60,000 PhDs in the SS
- By the end of the war, we have close to *a quarter million* PhDs in the SS.

So, while it is attractive to think of the SS as a bunch of ignorant goons, instead we find a highly educated, well trained membership with the mission of enforcing the "Final Solution".

3 The Warsaw Ghetto Uprising[27]

The story of the Warsaw Ghetto uprising has been well documented. But the details are often lost. There were *two* uprisings.

In January 1943, German SS and police began a wave of mass deportations, planning to send thousands of the ghetto's remaining Jews to forced-labor camps in the Lublin District of the General Government.

A small group of Jewish fighters, *armed with pistols*, infiltrated a column of Jews being forced to the *Umschlagplatz* (transfer point). At a prearranged signal, this group broke ranks and fought their German escorts. Although most of the Jewish fighters died in the battle, the attack disoriented the Germans, giving the Jews a chance to disperse.

Encouraged by the apparent success of the resistance, people in the ghetto began to construct subterranean bunkers and shelters. They were preparing for an uprising should the Germans attempt a final deportation of the remaining Jews from the ghetto.

Then, on April 19, 1943, the eve of the Passover holiday, the Jews of the Warsaw ghetto began the next act of armed resistance against the Germans. Lasting twenty-seven days, this act of resistance came to be known as the Warsaw ghetto uprising.

---

[26] Various sources
[27] The Holocaust Memorial Museum

The Holocaust Wars
They Didn't Go Quietly

And despite years in a starvation-menu ghetto and no access to weapons fought the Nazis for nearly a month, until artillery leveled the ghetto. It was a total modern Masada. Just unbelievable bravery against overwhelming odds with captured and handmade weapons. (This may have been where the lipstick-casing-as-cartridge-case story came from.)

<u>Some of the weapons used during the uprising.</u>[28]

Błyskawica was the backbone of the Polish underground weapons industry, along with the Polish version of the Sten submachine gun. Originally produced in Britain, the Błyskawica was covertly manufactured in mass numbers. It was designed by two Polish engineers, Wacław Zawrotny and Seweryn Wielanier, and it combined the exterior of a German MP-40 sub-machine gun and the interior mechanism of the British Sten. All parts of the weapon were joined with screws and threads, rather than bolts and welding.

Figure 16 - Polish soldier firing a Błyskawica during the Warsaw Uprising

Filipinka, also known as Perelka, was an unofficial name for ET *wz*. 40 hand grenades, manufactured in the Home Army underground facilities in 1940. It was designed by a former worker of the Rembertow Polish Army ammunition factory and based on a pre-war anti-tank grenade, model ET *wz*. 38. The designer was Edward Tymoszak, hence the ET abbreviation.

Figure 17 – Filipinka – right; Sidolowka – Left. By Halibutt – CC BY-SA 3.0

About 700 young Jewish fighters clashed with German forces, sometimes in hand-to-hand combat. These fighters were poorly equipped and lacked military training and experience. Yet they held the great German war machine, the masters of the blitzkrieg, at bay for 27 days. The effects of the diversion of these resources had significant impact on the German war effort.

It is grimly amusing to note that the Warsaw inmates, with their pathetic weaponry, held off the German army for 27 days, while the French army fell in 24 days.

4 Jewish Uprisings in the Camps
4.1 The Uprising in Treblinka

[29]On 2 August 1943, the prisoners at the Treblinka Extermination Camp, fearing that the camp would be dismantled, and the remaining prisoners killed, a resistance group within Treblinka organized a revolt. They seized arms, set camp buildings on fire, and rushed the main gate. Despite facing machine guns,

---

[28] Wikipedia
[29] United States Holocaust Memorial Museum

several hundred prisoners were able to break out of the camp. More than half were then traced and killed by Nazi authorities. Half remained at large.

4.2 Uprising at Sobibor

On October 14, 1943, prisoners in Sobibor killed 11 members of the camp's SS staff, including the camp's deputy commandant Johann Niemann.

A group of Polish Jews led by Leon Feldhandler formed a secret committee to plan a mass escape. However, its members lacked any military experience and made little progress.

When a group of Jewish Red Army POWs arrived in a transport from Minsk, the committee turned to them for advice. Lieutenant Alexander Pechersky developed a plan. The Soviet POWS would secretly kill some of the SS officials, taking their weapons and uniforms. Then, when the approximately 600 prisoners assembled for evening roll call, the POWs masquerading as camp personnel would kill the guards at the gate and on the towers. The revolt was set for a day when Sobibor's commandant would be away.

Close to 300 prisoners escaped, breaking through barbed wire and risking their lives in the minefield surrounding the camp. Only about 50 would survive the war.

4.3 Uprising at Auschwitz-Birkenau

Young Jewish women, like Ester Wajcblum, Ella Gärtner, and Regina Safirsztain, had obtained small amounts of gunpowder from the Weichsel-Union-Metallwerke, a munitions factory within the Auschwitz complex. This gunpowder was smuggled to the camp's resistance movement. Róza Robota, a young Jewish woman who worked in the clothing detail at Birkenau was one of the smugglers.

Under constant guard, the women in the factory stole small amounts of gunpowder, wrapped it in bits of cloth or paper, and then hid it on their bodies. They then passed it along the smuggling chain. Once she received the gunpowder, Róza Robota passed it to the *Sonderkommando*. The *Sonderkommando were a* special squad of prisoners who were forced to work in the camp's crematoria. Using this gunpowder, the leaders of the *Sonderkommando* planned to destroy the gas chambers and crematoria and then launch the uprising.

Figure 18 - Róza Robota, participant in the Auschwitz-Birkenau revolt of October 1944

On October 7, 1944, prisoners assigned to Crematorium IV at the Auschwitz-Birkenau killing center, the members of the *Sonderkommando* at Crematorium IV rose in revolt. The Germans crushed the revolt. Nearly 250 prisoners died during the fighting and guards shot another 200 after the mutiny was suppressed. Several days later, the SS identified four Jewish female prisoners who had been involved in supplying explosives to blow up the crematorium. All four women were executed.

But once again, the German war machine had to pause to deal with a Jewish uprising.

5 Partisans

The Holocaust Wars
They Didn't Go Quietly

5.1 What is a Partisan

From the Jewish Partisan Encyclopedia

> They were Jews in Europe, many of them teenagers, male and female, who fought against the Nazis during World War 2. The majority were regular folks who escaped the ghettos and work camps and joined organized resistance groups in the forests and urban underground.
>
> Some, like Polish teenager Frank Blaichman, knew their village would be turned into a ghetto; He escaped and joined a group of partisans in a forest. Others, like Abe Asner, were among the very few Jewish partisans with military training. Most partisans knew nothing about guns and ammunition, so people like Abe became important teachers and leaders.
>
> Less than ten percent of the partisans were women. Some were fighters and scouts; the majority were part of the vital infrastructure, cooking for the group and caring for the sick.

Jews who joined non-Jewish partisan groups often hid their Judaism because of antisemitism. Norman Salsitz, for example, used seven non-Jewish identities while fighting the Nazis and was able to save dozens of Jews from certain death.

5.2 What Defines Resistance

From the Jewish Partisan Encyclopedia

> Jewish resistance took on different forms. Physical resistance by the partisans was something that hurt the Germans. Spiritual resistance may not have affected the Germans and their collaborators directly, but it was important to the Jews, since the Nazis wanted to take away their dignity and self-respect.
>
> In defiance of the laws, the Jews held prayer services, or taught children to read Hebrew
>
> There were smugglers who sent children to safety and couriers who carried messages between the ghettos, as well as forgers who created documents for use in the outside world. Jews in the work camps sabotaged guns and other products they were making for the Germans.
>
> In Lithuania, Jewish partisans were responsible for significant damage to Nazi trains. Partisans also destroyed numerous Nazi power plants and factories, and focused their attention on other military and strategic targets, rather than on civilians.

Then there were the subtle forms of sabotage. The Nazis were focused on the use of slave labor, missing the fact that it would be easy to do hidden damage. From a book by John Diebold, Chief Scientist for Marine Operations in Norway

> In 1978 I worked with Norwegian colleagues during a US–Norwegian geophysical study of the Norwegian continental margin. For seismic sources, we used World War II surplus Nazi explosives which were stored in man-made caverns along Norwegian fjords.

> It was my personal observation that while the munitions dated 1939–1940 were reliable, those with dates from 1943 and later were typically weak or noneffective. This difference I ascribe either to intentional sabotage by the "Jews and concentration camp inmates" or to the simple substitution of inert materials for active ones by munitions plant managers, presumably due to the conflict between production quotas and availability of nitrates.

> Speer was apparently not above "production for production's sake" with a blind eye to quality control.

Then there was this incident reported by Richard J. Evans.

> A German bomb fell through the roof of my wife's grandmother's house in the East End of London in 1943 and lodged, unexploded, in her bedroom wardrobe. When the bomb disposal unit opened it up, they found a note inside. "Don't worry, English," it said, "we're with you. Polish workers."

This is resistance. This is courage.

Resistance and defiance took multiple manifestations. In her paper, "Tribute", Christina Sternberg chronicles many unique and touching stories. She will state that "a rather detailed indication of the actually massive resistance is provided by the paper by Jack Gostl entitled ""

5.3 Some Key Dates

Some key dates and events worth noting.

<u>July 20, 1941</u>

On July 20, 1941, the Germans order the establishment of a ghetto in Minsk. Jews in the ghetto form an underground resistance network in August 1941. Members of the underground set up a printing press and newspaper to distribute information to the ghetto population. The Jewish underground contacted outside partisans to find hiding places for Jews in the ghetto.

Members of the underground left the ghetto for the forests where they form partisan units and fight the Germans. The partisans in the forests worked to rescue Jews from the ghetto and bring them to the forests, where they establish partisan bases. Approximately 10,000 Jews flee the Minsk ghetto for the forests by 1944.

<u>January 1942</u>

The Jewish Army in France (Armee Juive; AJ), is established by Zionist youth groups in Toulouse, France. The AJ operates throughout France but is particularly active in the southern regions. Members are recruited from both Jewish and non-Jewish youth and resistance groups and are trained in military and sabotage activities. The AJ assassinates some of those who cooperate with the Germans and smuggles about 500 Jews and non-Jews across the border into neutral Spain.

The Holocaust Wars
They Didn't Go Quietly
January 21, 1942

In Vilna, after reports of mass killings of Jews at Ponary, outside Vilna, members of Zionist youth movements establish the United Partisan Organization (Fareynegte Partizaner Organizatsye, FPO) in the Vilna ghetto. The organization prepares to resist the Germans with sabotage and destruction. It establishes contact with other ghettos to acquire weapons and further encourage resistance. The last group of resistance fighters escapes the final destruction of the ghetto on September 23, 1943. They leave the ghetto through the sewers and join partisans in the Rudninkai and Naroch forests.

5.4 Where Did Jewish Partisans Fight

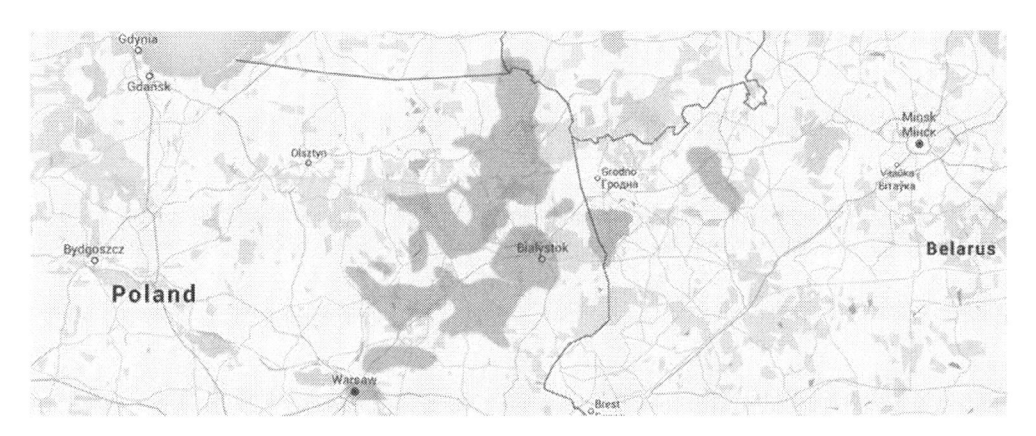

Figure 19 - Map of Jewish Partisan Fighting

Jewish partisans fought in almost every country in Europe. There was partisan activity in Belgium, Poland, Russia (Belarus and Ukraine), France, Italy, Greece and Lithuania. The partisans hid their encampments in the forests, swamps and mountains.

Partisan activity was particularly intense in Eastern Europe. Russian partisan units in Eastern Europe were highly organized and trained people to use guns, to dynamite bridges, and operate in a military fashion. Military order was kept in these groups (you could be shot for falling asleep on guard duty).

Partisans in Yugoslavia and Italy ambushed Nazi convoys and drew German attention away from the front. **Entire battalions were removed from the front lines to deal with the "partisan problem."** Entire battalions!

5.5 All Women Partisan Brigades
5.5.1 Introduction

The Holocaust Wars
They Didn't Go Quietly

I am particularly intrigued by the all-female partisans. It is indicative of the fact that the uprisings were not limited to "strong young men". The rebellious spirit was part of all of the Jewish victims. Some simply had more opportunity to use that spirit than others.

5.5.2 Russia (Vilna) Haika Grosman

Haika Grossman participated in the "movement" at a gathering in a convent near Vilna, where the group, led by Abba Kovner (1918–1988), decided on armed resistance. Sent to Bialystok to organize the fighting underground, she served as a contact person between Vilna and Bialystok and other ghettos. Her "ammunition" was resourcefulness, arrogance, courage, strong nerves and constant alertness, all of which saved her from virtually hopeless situations. "

Figure 20 - Haika Grossman

Between August 1943 and August 1944, Grosman participated in forming a group of six women in Bialystok, called "the anti-fascist committee." The aim of their hazardous activity was the ongoing maintenance of contact with the Soviet partisan brigade in the forest. They led Jews to them, established relations with anti-fascist Germans in the towns, and used their help to acquire ammunition for the underground and the partisans. With the surrender of the German troops, Grosman and her friends marched in the front line, side by side with the Soviet Brigade fighters that entered the city in August 1944.

5.5.3 Poland Eta Wrobel

In early 1940, Eta started working as a clerk in an employment agency. Soon she began resisting the occupation by forging false identity papers for Jews. In October 1942, Eta's ghetto was 'liquidated' and the Jews were exported to concentration camps. During the transition, Eta and her father managed to escape into the woods.

Figure 21 - Eta Wrobel

Eta organized an all-Jewish partisan unit of close to eighty people. Her unit stole most of their supplies, slept in cramped quarters, and had almost no access to medical attention. Eta's unit set mines to hinder German movement and to cut off supply routes.

The Holocaust Wars
They Didn't Go Quietly

5.5.4 Poland: Tosia Altman

Tosia Altman grew up in a Jewish Community in Lipno, Poland. She learned Polish and Hebrew and was an active member of the Ha-Shomer ha-Za'ir youth movement. With the outbreak of World War 2, she became a spy for Ha-Shomer ha-Za'ir. A fearless leader in the Jewish clandestine resistance to the Nazi occupation, Altman played an integral role in the Warsaw Ghetto uprising of April 18, 1943. She was badly injured in a fire in the attic in which she was hiding. Altman died a few months later in the custody of the Germans.

The leadership of Ha-Shomer ha-Za'ir in Vilna was extremely concerned with the fate of the movement's members who were left behind under German occupation. As a member of the central leadership, and with the appropriate personality and appearance, Altman was instructed to return to the Generalgouvernement (Nazi-occupied Poland). She was the first to return to occupied Poland (followed later by Josef Kaplan, Mordecai Anielewicz and Samuel Braslav).

Figure 22 - Tosia Altman

After two failed attempts to cross both the Soviet and German borders, she finally succeeded. Altman gathered the remaining youth-group leaders and organized the movement's branches. Even though Jews were prohibited from traveling on trains, Altman began to make the rounds of other cities. In every city she reached, she encouraged the young people to engage in clandestine educational and social activity. Altman corresponded with the leadership in Vienna (Adam Rand), the movement in Palestine and emissaries in Switzerland (Nathan Schwalb and Heine Borenstein). The correspondence was written in code for fear of German censors.

5.5.5 Hungary: Hannah Senesh

Born in Budapest, Hannah Szenes became a Zionist and immigrated to Palestine in 1939. In 1943 Jewish agency officials asked Szenes to join a clandestine military operation. She became a member of the Palmah and participated in a course for paratroopers.

In March 1944, she was dropped into Yugoslavia to aid anti-Nazi forces. Szenes was captured in June after entering Hungary, and sent to a prison in Budapest, where she was tortured. Since Szenes would not talk, Hungarian authorities arrested her mother. Both women remained silent. Given the chance to beg for a pardon in November 1944, Szenes instead chose death by firing squad.

Figure 23 - Hannah Szenes

5.6 Lithuania and Byelorussia

There were 850 Jews in the Lithuanian partisan movement. An additional 450 Jewish Lithuanian fighters in the Belorussian partisan movement and another 350 Lithuanian Jews in other groups brought the total to 1,650 Lithuanian Jews who fought as partisans. Of the 92 partisan battalions, Jews fought in the 22 that had sterling records in battle.

They Didn't Go Quietly

In 1943, Lithuanian Jewish partisans became unified under the direction of the Soviet Lithuanian partisan movement. The partisan movement was their only vehicle to fight actively against the Nazis. In some cases, all-Jewish units were formed within the larger organization of Lithuanian partisans.

Among their many successful missions, Lithuanian Jewish partisans derailed enemy trains, dynamited miles of train tracks, destroyed bridges, factories, water towers, and electrical transformers, and cut hundreds of miles of telephone and telegraph lines. In Vilna, they damaged the power station and sabotaged the water supplies. Other times they secured arms and food supplies.

Ten percent of the Lithuanian partisan population was comprised of Jewish partisans, but the units in which Jews served were responsible for 79% of the train derailments, 72% of the locomotives destroyed, and 22.9 % of the soldiers killed. Sabotage was only one their specialties. In total, 1,650 Jews took part in the resistance movement [as part of the] Lithuanian partisan movement. A total of 250 Jews were killed. Many received medals for their outstanding service.

The Holocaust Wars
They Didn't Go Quietly

6 Non-Resistance Resistance and the "Good Guys"

6.1 Introduction

It is our feeling that every discussion of the Holocaust requires a discussion of the "good guys", the non-Jews who stepped in and silently opposed the Nazis and rescued thousands of Jews.

6.2 Poland: Drs. Eugeniusz Lazowski and Stanislaw Matulewicz

In Rozwadow, Drs. Lazowski and Matulewicz (left) are credited with saving approximately 8,000 Jews by putting their medical knowledge to use. Having injected the town's Jews with a benign form of typhus he then informed the Nazis that an epidemic was at large. Terrified that it would spread, the Nazis quarantined the town and left it to its own devices. Known as 'the Polish Schindlers, the two of them saved 12 ghetto communities in this crafty manner. "I was not able to fight with a gun or a sword," Lazowski said. "But I was able to find a way to scare the Germans."

Figure 24 - Drs. Lazowski and Matulewicz (left)

6.3 Poland: Tadeusz Pankiewicz

- Within the Kraków Ghetto there were four prewar pharmacies owned by non-Jews. Tadeusz Pankiewicz was the only proprietor to decline the German offer of relocating to the gentile (non-Jewish) side of the city. He was given permission to continue operating his establishment as the only pharmacy in the Ghetto.

  The often-scarce medications and pharmaceutical products supplied to the ghetto's residents, often free of charge, substantially improved their quality of life. In effect, apart from health care considerations, they contributed to survival itself. In his published testimonies, Praniewicz makes particular mention of hair dyes used by those disguising their identities and tranquilizers given to fretful children required to keep silent during Gestapo raids.

Figure 25 - Tadeusz Pankiewicz

6.4 Poland: Irena Sendler

Another doctor, Irena Sendler, is credited with rescuing over 2,500 Jews from the Warsaw ghetto. Head of the children's section of Zegota – a secret organization that was a 'Council to Aid Jews'. Her actions aroused the attention of the Gestapo, and in 1943 she was arrested, tortured, and sentenced to death. A bribe saved her life, but nonetheless she was left unconscious in a forest, with both her arms and legs broken.

The Holocaust Wars
They Didn't Go Quietly

Appendix A – Jewish of US Medal of Honor Winners

The Congressional Medal of Honor is the highest military decoration an American service member can receive for outstanding heroism and bravery in battle. It is bestowed by the President upon a soldier in any of the branches of the U.S. Armed Forces who distinguish themselves through "conspicuous gallantry and intrepidity at the risk of his or her life above and beyond the call of duty."

The Medal of Honor has been awarded to 3,459 servicemembers.
At least 16 Jewish soldiers have been awarded the medal, 12 of them in the modern era.

World War I

- Sydney G. Gumpertz
- Benjamin Kaufman
- William Sawelson
- William Shemin

World War 2

- Isadore S. Jachman
- Ben Salomon
- Raymond Zussman

Korean War

- Leonard M. Kravitz
- Tibor Rubin

Vietnam War

- Jack H. Jacobs
- John L. Levitow

War in Afghanistan

- Christopher Celiz

© Copyright The Project Gideon Company - 2023

Appendix B – Righteous Among Nations

This is an honorific used by the State of Israel to describe non-Jews who for altruistic reasons risked their lives during the Holocaust to save Jews from extermination by the Nazis. As of 1 January 2021, the award has been made to 27,921 people. This table is not representative of the effort or proportion of Jews saved per country. These numbers are not necessarily an indication of the actual number of rescuers in each country, but rather it reflects the cases that were made available to Yad Vashem. This award is the Israeli equivalent of the United States Congressional Medal of Honor

Below is a partial list. Bear in mind that the named people had family and friends who were also placed in real danger. If these people were to also be counted, the list of honorees would number in the tens of thousands.

Country	Number of awards	Notable recipients
Poland	7,177	Jan Karski, Maria Kotarba, Irena Sendler, Irena Adamowicz
Netherlands	5,910	Frits Philips, Jan Zwartendijk
France	4,150	Anne Beaumanoir, Jeanne Brousse
Ukraine	2,673	Klymentiy Sheptytsky
Belgium	1,774	Queen Elisabeth of Belgium
Lithuania	918	Ona Šimaitė
Hungary	876	Endre Szervánszky, Sára Salkaházi
Italy	744	Giorgio Perlasca, Gino Bartali, Giuseppe Girotti, Odoardo Focherini
Germany	641	Oskar Schindler, Wilm Hosenfeld, Hans von Dohnanyi, Bernhard Lichtenberg

Figure 26 - Righteous Among Nations

I.4 WHAT IS UNIQUE / SINGULAR ABOUT "THE HOLOCAUST" EVENTS?

OPINION PIECE GENERATED

BY "PROJECT GIDEON COMPANY ('PGC")

TO BE SHORTLY LAUNCHED

I.   Author's Background -- Pre-U.S.A 77

II. Author's Background -- In U.S.A 79

III. The Holocaust (Crime, Criminals, Wars) 84

Written By:

Jacob Sternberg ("JS")

© PGC, 2023

The Holocaust Wars
What is Unique

I. <u>Author's Background</u> – <u>Pre–U.S.A.</u>
Jacob Sternberg ("JS") born 6/15/1938 in Warsaw, Poland
Wrong time, Wrong place
- He is a confirmed Holocaust survivor, some trauma (hunger, cold, fear) – no camps – just hiding

- Claims to have completely recovered from the experience
  Recovered by heroic parents' efforts <u>and by</u> intense classical education (languages, math, science) provided by university professors <u>and by</u> "Jewish studies" provided by a Rabbi tutor. [6 hours/day, 6 days/week, for three years]. Father, as a smuggler in Salzburg, Austria, generated the funds for this luxury.

- Claims to have been blessed by the <u>"Israel Effect" that lasted a long lifetime.</u>
  The 12-year stay in Israel (end 1948 to mid-1960), provided the following:

  - Exceptional private schooling. He became president of a 600-student body.
    Due to prior education, he was first in all the classes he attended.
  - Highly disciplined youth organization stressing morals, excellence in any chosen task performance, patriotic Jew mindset and all the Marxism he could inhale.
  - Membership in a kibbutz which took effort to adjust to.
  - Prior to joining the Israeli Army (1956), extensive training (provided by the military to "Promising youth") in flying gliders ((imagine a Polish glider; Vorona and Piper cub planes (ages 15-18), training included weaponry and survival.
  - In the four-year military service (1956-1960) he served as:
    * A paratroop officer for two years (and a military intel officer on the Syrian and Gaza borders)
    * Participated in multiple actions on all Israeli borders. He was fortunate enough to

serve under exceptional commanders which significantly affected his dedication to objectives he chose to undertake.

●●● He claims that Hell will freeze over before JS thinks of himself as a "victim."

The Holocaust Wars
What is Unique

What is Unique …. (Continued)

II. <u>JS Background – in U.S.A.</u>

Starting with arrival in 9/1960 and lasting to date, JS has been blessed in all the 62 years he spent in this country. As it turns out, the above is important in numerous ways which we shall explore in this opinion piece.

- <u>The "U.S. Effect"</u>

A detailed life story, provided in a memoir written by JS (titled "Jacob's Odyssey") tells the following:

- Everything in America is massive, big, loud, chaotic and almost worth bragging about. Bragging is not just prevalent in Texas (where they could easily classify their swimming pools as the flushing mechanism for their toilets …).

- The memoir's stories of immense luck <u>are riveting</u>:

  * The dean at City College violated administrative rules and had JS matriculate at CCNY

  * The first employer "Premier Research Labs" had JS salary doubled <u>twice</u> when JS found critical math error – all in the first three months.

  * Within six years of arrival (in 1960) **he became a professor.**

  * Two years later (1968) he built his first high tech company and thereafter became an inventor and CEO of high-tech companies.

  * Although he had no technological failure, JS didn't exactly know nor sufficiently respect "business physics." In America, you pay a price for disrespecting "business physics," such as "falling in love" with projects you should skip. However, eventually, the vast experiences, chronicled as case studies, in a JS-written book ("The Ride on America's Business Highway") toughened this immigrant and led to a productive and an interesting life.

The Holocaust Wars
What is Unique

- Many factors drove JS to become the architect of a major Holocaust related project ("Better defined as Mega Project") – the most complex undertaking of his entire long life. You will know what attracted JS after we tell you about the project and the company to get it done.

One would imagine that somewhere in the vast data reservoirs lie the answers to the three questions: What/How/Why did it happen.

More than that, the first two (What/How) are not extraordinarily difficult, it is the "Why" that provides the bellyache.

It is exactly when enormous data volumes vastly overwhelm you and confusing uncertainties raise their ugly head, <u>that it is exactly the time to put on the tight shoes</u>. They hurt much but they focus you to concentrate on the happy moment that you can take the shoes off after concentrating on some (even tiny) victory and ignoring irrelevant factoids. Please note that JS intends to follow this awful suggestion. He also ran a Tel Aviv marathon (in Purim, 1986) with a sprain, a well swollen ankle. His runner number was 100.

He finished the run in 4:01 hours and enjoyed taking the tight shoes off.

There is no secret in how you do it.

You worry so much about how you make each step that you forget to watch the signs telling you how much you have already covered in distance. The first he realized the importance of this idea was at mile 24 of this race. And "2 miles to go" became a cinch.

The above marathon run illustration, (sprained ankle and tight shoes) tells how a relatively sane person justifies undertaking tough projects.

The Holocaust Wars
What is Unique

One would imagine that somewhere in the vast data reservoirs lie the answers to the three

questions: What/How/Why did it happen.

More than that, the first two (What/How) are not extraordinarily difficult, it is the "Why" that

provides the bellyache.

It is exactly when enormous data volumes vastly overwhelm you and confusing uncertainties raise their ugly head, <u>that it is exactly the time to put on the tight shoes.</u> They hurt much but they focus you to concentrate on the happy moment that you can take the shoes off after concentrating on some (even tiny) victory and ignoring

irrelevant factoids. Please note that JS intends to follow this awful suggestion. He also ran a Tel Aviv marathon (in Purim, 1986) with a sprain, a well swollen ankle. His runner number was 100.

There is no secret in how you do it.

You worry so much about how you make each step that you forget to watch the signs telling

you how much you have already covered in distance. The first he realized the importance of

this idea was at mile 24 of this race. And "2 miles to go" became a cinch.

The above marathon run illustration, (sprained ankle and tight shoes) tells how a relatively sane person justifies undertaking tough projects.

The Holocaust Wars
What is Unique

III. The Holocaust (Crime, Criminals, Wars)

III.1 The Monumental Research Re Holocaust is a Fact.

- Hell should also freeze over if the following facts are not acknowledged and lauded to the end of days …

1. The largest, most thorough, research project ever, has generated near-infinite data covering what happened in the Holocaust events (1939-1945).

   - The project is worldwide, encompassing stellar academic, governmental, social and civic institutions engaging literally thousands of competent/stubborn researchers.
   - In addition to collecting, authenticating, storing and mining the data and analyzing the information gleaned from such mining, numerous educational materials are generated and widely disseminated.
   - Imagine one such researcher, say Rich Bronstein, at the "Yad Vashem" (a stellar Holocaust research institution in Jerusalem)) who has the expertise that will sharpen your understanding of films in general and for about 450 "Holocaust Films" as a special category that will – nearly by definition – teach what a powerful tool film could be in focusing on historic monumental events. By most likely viewing all the about 450 "Holocaust Films," he segregates about 50 of such films that satisfy his selected criteria of "worthy films." In an incredible book he informs you that every year and a half a new "Holocaust film" pops out of the Hollywood factory and provides you with an interesting statistic that the worthiness of a Holocaust film popping is just about in the 11% category that the massive film factories produce as worthy films, applies to Holocaust ones. The added benefit that Brownstein provides to the films' world is the guts to critique stellar films and filmmakers who don't satisfy his extreme criteria for verifying the veracity of eyewitnesses. After all, "What an eyewitness sees depends on where he stands." Imagine attacking Spielberg. I, a former paratroop officer and pretender to having "guts" and warrior skills and mentality,

may not actually dare to do. I also have developed the phobia of not entering a cemetery at midnight...
- We should all be cognizant that the collected facts may be impeccable and yet, the analytical conclusion may be less than perfect.

III.2 <u>Everything About the Holocaust is Unique</u>

- The author believes that everything connected to the Holocaust is unique/singular. This simply means that:

2. <u>Pre-Existing conditions</u> coagulated to generate <u>The Biggest Crime</u> in history against the Jews by virtue of what the Nazis did to Jews.
3. <u>Pre-Existing conditions</u> generated <u>The Biggest Crime</u> in history against humanity by virtue of how they executed the crimes against Jews, designated "subhumans" and slave laborers.
4. A Malignant State of Mind resulting from near theological beliefs of the Nazi cult in a Totalitarian/Deterministic/Utopia that allows "using all means necessary" to commit the biggest crimes. By virtue of its malignancy, this state of mind may not permit a rational explanation of <u>why the crimes were committed.</u>

- The Pre-Existing conditions, when aggregated are unique/singular by generating <u>the worst century in human history – the 20th Century</u> – unlike any other.
- Just a cursory peak at history is sufficient to justify (to a reasonable degree) the above beliefs. This opinion paper is aimed to justify the author's assertions above, among others. <u>A quick peak at the 20th Century pre WWII will be helpful.</u>

5. At the beginning of the 20th Century, some empires were collapsing (Ottoman, Habsburg, Czarist Russia). Some "empires to be" (unified Germany) were looking to be new colonies owner. Older empires ran out of gas (Spain, Portugal, Dutch, ...). The big empires were looking for serious expansion (G. Britain, France).
6. The First World War ("WWI") made many regions on the glove ungovernable (MidEast, North Africa, East Europe and

Russia, in particular). Every power lost the flower of their youth, population were uprooted and the nominal winners assumed the normal Imperialist posture of severely punishing the losing German Imperial-wannabe. Small scale Totalitarian dreamers' revolution encouraging numerous revolutionary aspirants worldwide.

7. A big economic depression worldwide added fuel to left/right revolution-like kerfuffles, hopeful colonials created severe difficulties to their empires' problems (involving getting impoverished).

THE WORLD GOT INTO IDEAL READINESS FOR A MOTHER OF ALL WARS – WWII.

- A quick peak at a much earlier history could add a reasonable idea of really different events – very different from Holocausts.

In the real "olden days" jousting between empires resulted in parading the slaved losers and some booty triumphantly. Many hundred years back, religious and colonial wars allowed conversions and surrender by losers to save their lives. No such choices were available to Holocaust-entangled Jews. "History is a foreign country; they did things differently there." (Hartley, British Writer)

- To grasp the uniqueness of all the aspects of "The Holocaust" (as the author claims), add to the pre-existing conditions a quick examination of "The Holocaust" as a descriptive term to a particular set of events.

Many atrocities have been committed in the past. These were designated as pogroms, genocides, mass killings and several other ways.
<u>Only one has "earned" the designation of "Holocaust."</u>

The Holocaust Wars
What is Unique

The reasons for the uniqueness of this designation are quite known.

8. "Holocaust" involves <u>Extermination of Jews</u> as a race. At every stage of extermination, the events were accompanied by extreme humiliation, unusual hatred, unprecedented softening of the potential resistance urge via starvation and terror, all preceded by unusual levels of preparation and planning (far exceeding exterminations of rats …)

9. Although atrocities were committed against Roma people, homosexuals, mentally disabled and other Nazi designated "subhumans," none were <u>LEGALLY</u> in the preferred extermination category. None were part of an extended Rube-Goldberg administrative labyrinth of feeding the active extermination camps with predictable arrivals from feeder installations.

10. No other set of events has involved the enormous price tag attached to the extermination of Jews.
    It is a demented choice in all the four fronts of WWII
    In the of face of severe manpower, materials (e.g., steel, chemicals) and (yes) fuel shortages.
    Picked the war on Jews as a major undertaking, <u>as the fourth front.</u>

11. No other set of events illustrates, better than the following example, the malignant/demented mindset of the "perps":

    "British troops were advancing on Neuengamme [a labor camp in Northern Germany]. <u>Hitler has committed suicide a few days earlier</u>, SS Chief Heinrich <u>Himmler has given orders not to surrender the camps with their prisoners.</u>

Guards put 8,000 inmates onto two ships, the Cap Arcona and the Thielbeck. On May 3, a British Air Force squadron, knowing nothing about the ships cargo, bombed and sank them" – The El Paso Times "Retracing a Lost Life 12/18/2006."

The Nazis knew that the German warships will be sunk. And imagine: the camp commanders even violated SS Commander's orders.

12. The same deranged mindset was in full bloom when the vaunted industrial sector (e.g., I.G. Farben Conglomerate) has embraced a joint venture with the SS to employ slave labor to serve their multi-front war. The demented/malignant idea that emaciated/sick/tortured and humiliated laborers could produce adequate war products was only exceeded by the sicker idea that dead or incapacitated laborers can be replaced and retained in a continuous huge logistical effort competing for resources with military necessities.

The Holocaust Wars
What is Unique
The Holocaust (Crime, Criminals, Wars)

<u>We barely covered</u> the issue of uniqueness of "The Holocaust" by reviewing pre-existing conditions for the mega crime and some aspects of the demented/malignant mindset of the perps. This is the point where we adopt some non-orthodox, non-consensus views no matter what the experts say.

III.3   To question the near orthodox view of the Holocaust's facts (what and how it all happened), we postulate:

    III.3.1   The orthodox, "near consensus" view of the Holocaust is:

    At best, incomplete, <u>AND AT WORST</u>, faulty in some serious respects.

- <u>The incomplete, "near consensus" definition</u>

  [A serious objective of PGC – the company that will shortly be launched – is to assist ourselves and anybody else – big and small, to "nail down" the facts and the causes that made the Holocaust happen.]

  The popular view simply states: "The Holocaust is a set of events whereby six million European Jews were killed by the Nazis in German-held territories during 1939-1945 ongoing World War II."

  More "sensitive" and detailed version adds
  A time correction: "Primarily from end of 1941 till mid 1945"

A judgement correction: "Under severe maltreatment under brutal and humiliating conditions"

Added information: "Subverting conquered peoples to participate in atrocious attacks on Jews conducted by their youth.

Unless, <u>once and for all</u>, we adopt a major correction, the consensus adherents will confuse themselves and everybody else.

- <u>PGC's Suggested ("Less Consensus") View of "The Holocaust </u>(A Draft …)

"The Holocaust is the <u>Final Set of Events</u> in a long, 2000-year sequence of <u>pogroms, atrocities and genocides directed specifically at Jews</u> in Asia, North Africa and Europe.

<u>Being directed at Jews as a "Race,"</u> it <u>culminated in the extermination</u> of six million European Jews in regions ruled by Germany in World War II ("WWII"), primarily between year-end 1941 and mid-1945.

<u>It is a singular event</u>, which unlike any other massive killing event, involved enormous allocations of resources in a multi-front war, meticulous planning due to significant shortages of fuel and raw materials, shortage of manpower and required continental size handling of difficult logistics.

It was, worst of all, <u>executed by a cult</u>, stubbornly clinging to a near-theological belief's flimsy excuse for unprecedented hatred, utmost humiliation and maximum pain accompanying exterminations.

In its wake, it left a seriously disoriented Jewish survivor population (in the millions), a vast number of non-Jewish people of honor who couldn't grasp a country gone berserk, a strange and sick admiration for the Holocaust implementor's detailed orderliness (ya, ordnung …), paving the way for a smart imitator who "cloaked" subjugation of peoples with Totalitarian/Utopian 'Kool Aid.' Subjugation dictators, although like Stalin and Mao, are responsible for tens of millions of dead, they missed the "Holocaust" designation even though their foul deeds lasted for 46 long years ((1945-1991) for the Soviets and, these days, continued by China.

There is much that can be added – we leave it to phenomenally equipped major institutions.

We cling to the above as a minimum because we wish to highlight that:

The Holocaust Wars
What is Unique

The number of dead Jews far exceeds 6,000,000 if the past "comes marchin in." the damage to three generations of Jews is huge and cannot be easily estimated. The refuse is still smelly in the European sewer AND, the appeasers still are eager for Iran to have the bomb and really get Armageddon going. The sheriff that guarded the Europeans' bacon for the whole century is now tired.

To make the above assertions stick, PGC has generated research papers that deal with further suggestions we have as provided just below.

To present the uniqueness of the criminals in the Holocaust arena, PGC generated a set of research papers.

These papers are part of a mega project which was generated and methodically executed in over 20 years. At a glance, please note that:

- The foundation for the mega project is an available, "Knowledge Base" consisting of:
    - Key Primary manuscripts   -- True Life Stories
    - Multiple Companion Manuscripts -- True and not farfetched fictional plots to buttress the primary Manuscripts
    - Film and play plots planned at various stages
    - White papers – Advocating formation of PGC, defining its mission, implementation plans for achieving
    - The mission, background and assessment of PGC
    - Media coverage of key characters' achievements
    - PGC critiques

The above categorized Knowledge Base is presented in the mega projects ("THE HOLOCAUST WARS BOOKS").

The Holocaust Wars
What is Unique

The above data was presented, at the early stage, to tell more than a hint, that PGC is serious AND, on the day of its launch, PGC will have a vast volume of data, information and intelligence which it will own and be ready to supply adequate/insightful/respectful Holocaust Memorial products to assure that the Memorial is not one long crying event but is balanced by a tsunami of heroic events and achievements as a companion to the sad story that will be told.

WE CAN NOW REVERT BACK TO ATTACKING THE PERPS.

The Holocaust (Crime, Criminals, Wars) Continued

III.4 The Criminals

The near-consensus view of the Holocaust quite properly identifies the Totalitarian Nazi regime as the responsible perp (we use the term to underline disgust). It is, of course, correct. However, it misses the most important conclusion one could/should derive from the Holocaust events study – THE NAZIS WEREN'T ALONE.

This assertion consists of:

- The 2000-year continuous atrocities specifically against Jews (spread all over the world) having relatively short respites AND (every so often), the many blood libels invented, made the Jews a loathsome tribe and an "enemy." The crusaders, for instance, practiced their fighting skills by killing Jews on the way to Jerusalem's liberation. Not only did the Jews "Kill the son of God," have childrens' blood on their matza on Passover, always be and behave as "foreigners" nearly everywhere, and seemingly have horns after sundown and, of course, wanting to take over the world [as the czars concocted the "elders of Zion" accusation that stuck]. Hating and hurting Jews became somewhat of a sport. The Nazi-conquered regions had their own dislike of Jews…

- The European convulsions (political and economic) with a WWI disrupting lives and beliefs, followed by worldwide depression, the wildfire spread of Totalitarian cockroaches (also fueled by the Communist "Kool Aid," so willingly consumed). The failure of the League of Nations created the ability for Nazis to overwhelm the equally aggressive leftist coalition in Germany.

Totalitarians always signal their utopian action plans – nobody in the "Democratic Europe" did anything to counter the Nazi rise and their visible actions fully disclosing their intentions. It is reasonable to assume that France alone could have eaten the Nazi regime for breakfast prior to 1936.

The appeaser possessed an unending supply of "Criminal Naivete" and, as Hemingway said, "Stupidite."

- The PGC's papers re the role of the Psychiatric and Eugenicists cartels indicate:

(1.) Although PGC's papers didn't invent the important effect that these geniuses had an important role in the conception and the execution of Holocaust crimes, PGC wants to show how effective these cartels were.

If PGC's emphasis is correct, then we ask:

(2.) Why didn't these cartels' have a huge presence in the Nuremberg Trials docks?
Why weren't these cartels' geniuses captured and been prevented (many of them) from arrival in the U.S.?

(3.) PGC's papers present the data. <u>Why is it not widely known</u> that the SS was crawling with Ph.Ds. in all the pseudo sciences? Why is it that the popular consensus suggests that the Nazis were just "brutal dimwits diseased with unnatural obedience to stupidly barked orders?"

PGC, in its desire to have <u>a Knowledge Base that evades nothing</u>, we even deal with the dilemma of having the U.S. benefit from Von Braun and all, knowing what they did to strengthen the loathsome regime they were plucked from.

PGC asserts that the criminals involved in the Holocaust events come from many countries and derive criminality from every geopolitical view and social ranking. This vast array of culprits differ only in the level of criminality they inflicted. Think of it as a pyramid.

<u>At the Base</u> the widest part of the pyramid – are the people who for a multiplicity of reasons, believe in utopia of some sort, run by utopians' Avant guard who know what is good for the masses in dire need to rapidly change, via revolt and revolution, the existing political/economic/cultural conditions. Their "Kool Aid" to be drunk consists of bravely spreading the idea that the nasty rulers need replacement NOW and "by all means necessary." This base accounts for most people who emerged from the Middle Ages, tasted (via education) the excitement of knowing things, relaxed a bit from very strict religious dogma BUT DIDN'T MAKE IT TO THE VERY PRIVILEGED (AND THE VERY RICH), even though some of the offspring of very privileged joined the revolutionaries.

The Holocaust Wars
What is Unique

Professor Talmon in his "Totalitarian Democracy" books explains the above much better.

- In the middle layers – a sizeable one, yet smaller than the base – are the people who for religious and cultural reasons can't accept the ideas provided by the "Kool Aid" dispensers. It also includes many who entered the capitalist system, made a line above subsistence, and who succeed to peel off some dreaming privileged to enable an economic and social system without "hanging too many people." This is the layer that creates appeasers and engages in "criminal naivete."

- Next layer above – a layer smaller than the middle one consists of the collection of highly ambitious former important members of either of the two other layers. These are solely interested in their own "success" (economics and power).

- The top layer consists of charismatic few leaders which we will focus on.

- The top of the criminal pyramid are the rare powerful personalities whose effect on their nations and on their victims is far beyond imagination.

- Of the worst trio ever (Hitler/Stalin/Mao) Hitler is the biggest "achiever" ever. PGC expects to precisely define why this Oscar belongs to this malignant one. Stalin and Mao killed more people than Hitler. Thus, the Oscar is not due for body count. Stalin impacted more nations and peoples' destinies than either of his competitors. All three demonstrated how to "devour their own nations" (a biblical expression) and affect the others to march to hell.

- Hitler was a strategic idiot. Adam Tooze primarily and others have pointed out how insanity/derangement and stupidity guided a Germany-sector war (with extermination of Jews as a fourth front). How delays got his generals flustered in the Russian front, and how fuel and materials shortages impacted the vaunted wisdom of his brilliant generals.

The Holocaust Wars
What is Unique

- Stalin took a huge agrarian country stitched of multiple nationalities that couldn't get a crop prediction right into a war of technological and economic titans, committing huge crimes worldwide just after the war, and unleashing a Third World War that lasted 46 years (1945-1991). However, none of his crimes rose to Holocaust level. (He even helped form Biro Bijan – a "Jewish State" in the Far East and after all, he was an aspiring theology student).

- Mao was probably the "Big Dead Body Count Champ" in the trio. As a strategic genius, he predicted and worked to realize the 100-year plan which the current leadership will work hard to make happen by 2049. However, notice what Mao did. He unleashed millions of psychotic youngster batch holding up Mao's Red Book to harass a billion of older citizens in a constant revolutionary fervor and melting anything of metal for the glory of the revolution. While the constant revolution is ongoing, Uyghurs, Tibetans and others are subjected to the old Totalitarian depravities of Mao's making.

It is quite sad that Obama's "Business Wife" admired Mao "Because he did it his way." What Brilliance!

The Lesser Totalitarians

PGC asserts that the criminal contingent associated with the Holocaust is quite sizeable. The 20th Century geopolitical events unmask some ugly actors at the WWII start.

13. Germany has bombers flying on missions for Franco in Spain. It showed that the European Democracies tolerated it. Same no response was not even contemplated with Italian Atrocities in Ethiopia and Japanese in Manchuria.

The Holocaust Wars
What is Unique

14. Hitler was dumb enough, thank God, to drop Franco from his coalition with Mussolini and Hirohito. All Franko wanted was a voice in managing North African oil.

15. One only needs to read Hemingway's <u>Analysis of the French</u> pre and at the Start of World War II – "<u>Vénalité and Stupidité</u>" were added to their famous slogan. Incredible incompetence of the French leadership can make these venerated perps as contributors to the Holocaust. The fact that verifies the assertion re the French is their refusal to give their entire assembled fleet in North Africa to the Allies – necessitating the sinking of the entire armada. <u>Who the Hell gave the French a seat at the "Winners' Table" when WWII ended?</u>

16. Most of the European governments who quickly collapsed upon short or no resistance to the German Blitzkriegs onslaught have adopted the infamous Nuremberg Laws – What happened to these leaders? PGC wants to, and will extend best efforts to enlarge this knowledge. At present, PGC has sufficient evidence to make the assertions. Some of these European countries had entire division strength units in military actions and guard duties at various camps, in the service of the Nazis.

One major criminal involved in the Holocaust events is difficult to "Nail Down." Difficult or not, PGC will try. The major research institutions know the facts but may be reluctant to assign negative deeds and views to the Soviet Union because the Soviets were an important and capable force helping to defeat the Nazis.

The Holocaust Wars
What is Unique

There are identifiable four distinct periods in Soviet Holocaust involvement:

1. (<u>1917-1939</u>) is a period where the soviets were penetrating Western intelligence agencies and political parties and unions for both aggressive and defensive reasons (the Soviets have been quite analytical and capable to exert influence within the feckless League of Nations and other international organizations. They had reasonable (viewed from their perch) defensive actions to minimize Western enmity. The Soviets were particularly successful in organizing colonies' urge to become independent from mother empires.

    – From a view of Holocaust analysis, the Soviets contributed quite handsomely to European Democracies' (Britain and France in particular) misunderstanding of the capabilities of a rearmed and revenge-seeking Germany. <u>Appeasement flourishes when naivete of high order reigns.</u> The criminal naivete allowed dillydallying with preparedness for war by France and its neighbors. It was exhibited with the Anschluss of Austria in 1938 and German occupation of previously ceded territories.

2. (<u>9/1939 – 6/1941</u>) is a second period in the Soviet role in the Holocaust. The West has been relatively surprised by the announced Molotov/Ribbentrop Agreement.
    – The German calculation was straightforward: The Blitzkrieg in Western Europe could proceed without worrying about the potential Russian front in the East. And a rapid closure in Western Europe, North Africa could "Taken care of" and oil will be plentiful. The Soviets provided a <u>strategic gift</u> to the perps. Controlling Western Europe will thus allow two simultaneous goals to

be gained: (1) Beat the hated Communists in a major battle royale to come and, most importantly (2) Exterminate the Jews who pose an existential threat to the 1000-year Reich.

- The Soviet calculation was simple: Let the blood flow from huge German and Western European

  empires casualties – for Russia, it is a Big Tactical Gift. They knew, because they are smart [The author knows this as a fact and provides the evidence to back it up], that at some not distant future, Germany will turn on them. By that time, the war will be costly to both Soviet enemies and mother Russia will be able to, at least defend itself and, at best, increase its European penetration and, "God willing," succeed in Africa and Asia.

  As a result of the agreement, Germany will control Poland and the Soviets will control the Baltic States.

- A "Funny Thing Happened on the Way to the Forum" (said Zero Mostel). The Germans were implementing the infrastructure for Jews' extermination – herd Jews into ghettos, transit camps, live-testing extermination processes and started to kill Polish intelligencia AND encourage anti-Jewish outbreaks everywhere. The Russians "Sovietized" the economies of the Baltic states. These states didn't take kindly to the harsh measures of Sovietization. The population noticed that many Jews residing in there, and quite a sizeable portion, that had escaped from Nazi controlled Poland have favored being "Sovietized" than killed, became a hated target of the Baltic states' irate population, which describes why Jews were not popular. When the Russians Sovietized Ukraine in the 1930s, causing enormous starvation and millions of dead, have caused enormous animosity toward Jews who were perceived as Soviet supporters.

3. (<u>6/1941 – 5/1945</u>) is a third phase of Soviet relation with Jews.
    - The Soviets were welcoming Jews who escaped from German occupied Poland and moved many of them to safety in Russia's east.
    - The Soviets fought like lions against the immense German onslaught on Russia and provided considerable support to many organized partisan groups who provided a strong headache to German commanders.
    - Under dictat of expediency, the Allies welcomed the Russian entry into the fray and extended immense support to Russian insatiable needs of materials.
    - The sympathy towards Russia in the West was increasing as the tide was turning against the Germans in numerous ways. The sympathy was reflected in Western Allies tolerance of Russian behavior when regimes changed in the lands they liberated (e.g., early setup of East Germany – their "window" to the East. The Russians increased their worldwide espionage activities which eventually provided them with nuclear capabilities, significant presence in Asia and Africa.

    Eventually, Russia was able (as Khruschev boasted in the late 50's) to seriously threaten to bury the dirty capitalists. The Russians succeeded to cobble together the "Warsaw Pact," the strong Bandung Alliance of non-aligned countries and support numerous colonies seeking to leave their mother empires.

    It became clear that the anti-Western alliances increased potency allowed numerous dictators in the Russian orbit, on all continents, to support a new threat of eventual revolutionary socialism push to affect geopolitical changes.

Although Russia supported the formation of Israel, they just wished to create a headache for U.S. and all its allies by MidEast shenanigans which had, as the Russians predicted, numerous detrimental effects on the West. We deal with this issue below. Israel was not supposed to win all those wars.

4. (1945-1991) is a fourth phase in Soviet relations with Jews and Israel. The MidEast is Exhibit A to insane/byzantine wars that make no sense to their participants and everyone else.

   – The Iran/Iraq War was just a jousting between two idiotic/fanatic regimes. Iraq wanted to show off its 11,000 generals (kid you not) and Iran – the urgently and strong wisher for early Armageddon wanted to show ??? all embedded in slogans "Death to America" and "Final Solution" to Israel.

   A more thorough examination of Iran under the Ayatollahs discloses surprising insanity that helps PGC to consider that the Holocaust may not be totally over. Several opinion pieces combine with critiques are part of the Knowledge Base.

   In all the wars between Arab League coalitions and Israel, Russia was an unrelenting supplier of advanced weapons <u>AND</u>, in several of the wars, Russia credibly threatened with direct military intervention (by paratroop divisions).

- The insane wars between Arab neighbors (Iraq/Kuwait), (Egypt/Libya), (Algeria/Morocco), pale compared to the fully idiotic Saudi "brilliancy" to QUADRUPLE the price OPEC charges for oil in one day in 1973. It looked loony in 1973 and it was the obvious notice to the U.S. to achieve energy independence.

  The Soviet Union's collapse in 1991 (for reasons PGC tries to explain in its Knowledge Base) DID NOT BRING TO AN END THE RUSSIAN MEDDLING IN THE MIDEAST — Invariably to the detriment of Israel.

- PGC attempts to explain a lethal combination of Russian unbending connections to Syria and Iraq, run by imbeciles, Russian bases in Syria, the insane/artificial high cost of fossil fuels, continuing appeasement policy towards a fully aggressive Russia.

  The changing MidEast and Russian incompetence may suggest factors to diminish the danger that is posed by a nuclear Iran, an asylum country (N. Korea) and the awful Chinese mother of the asylum's patient.

  More on this, check the Knowledge Base.

III.5 The Holocaust Wars

Not all wars involve physical weapons, some "Intellectual" wars are meaner and more criminally bent than physical wars.

The mean "Intellectual" wars can leave a wake of awful ideological imprints in mind and psyche with lasting effects.

The Holocaust wars had both types of wars occur simultaneously and the wake is still smelly.

The Holocaust Wars
What is Unique

PGC classifies the set of wars surrounding the Holocaust as follows:

- The "Intellectual Wars" to define what/how and why did the Holocaust happen.
- The physical wars involved in the extermination of Jews
- The intellectual wars, post Nazis' defeat
- The physical wars, post Nazis' defeat
- The potential physical wars in the near future

- PGC has undertaken the very "tall" task of clarifying the facts and conjectures for each category and help the Jewish memory bank <u>AND</u> the humanity's memory bank accept deposits of plans, intellectual products and suggested management of practical implementation processes so that, in the future, dividends will flow that minimize the repetition of atrocities of multiple kinds.

    Exhibiting a bit of melodrama, PGC claims that the "tall" task is really more complicated, more difficult to make the solid deposits than so far stated. <u>To be practical</u>, we start with the need – which PGC claims is imperative – <u>win the first intellectual war</u> and deposit this win.

III.5.1 <u>The First Intellectual War</u>

- The Knowledge Base provides the reasoning behind the need to win the high ground in the definition of "The Holocaust."

- Occupying the high ground means adopting essentially PGC's definition. It is logical to assume that the major institutions with their expertise in the relevant history and sociology disciplines will make appropriate modifications without destroying the fundamental idea.

- The enemies of the "PGC-like" definition are numerous and vocal because they can imagine what follows the adoption of such a definition. Among the enemies are a large mix of:

    All Totalitarian states who are singled out as the midwives of sizeable atrocities. These constitute the majority of the U.N. – pretending to be "A World Government."

    Almost all aggrieved U.N. members who object to the Jewish central role because their pain is not heard and the Jews "suck out the air" and theirs are not acknowledged and acted upon.

From the above, the most vocal and influential enemies will be the major up and coming powers:

China, which is already a superpower and a criminal in committing atrocities (against Tibetans, Uyghurs and other minorities), India, Brazil and a host of African and Asian large Totalitarians with blood on their hands.

PGC advocates to having the Centennial Memorial very far away from the U.N. and provides the reasons for this recommendation.

III.5.2 The Second Intellectual War

Directly tied to the first war, the second is an internal Jews vs. Jews war. There exists a host of strong Jewish organizations, many with strong ("muscular") and dedicated membership, very adept at infighting with other organizations for position and turf, financial ability to lobby and capable management.

Some of the internal kerfuffles are trivial, but some are not.

Even though PGC is not an expert in this arena, it is not hard to identify serious rifts that need to be handled. Among these:

Jewish organizations who believe that Israel is an "Apartheid Country." As such, it should be sanctioned under a "BDS" policy (Boycott, Disinvest, Sanction). These organizations are in close contact with several non-trivial groups in Israel whose support provides anti-Israel and anti-Jewish organizations worldwide as "proof" of Israel's criminality.

Jewish organizations whose anti-Israel bend is rooted in geopolitical issues of (a) A two state solution (b) The strong Capitalist economic direction under right wing governments in Israel (c) Anti-Netanyahu phobia, similar to anti-Trump strong attitudes in the U.S. (d) Anti-religions bend which attacks the religious justification of settlements.Jewish organizations who actually really loath the above groups and want to send them to Madagascar or worse.

Jews should remember, "So Spake PGC," that the shtetl Chelm, "Known for its funny fools," having only <u>30,000 or less Jews had five newspapers, multiple social services organizations</u>, an active Jewish and secular education, at least three political organizations and, even being poor (12-hour workday), had sport teams and active Jewish life. Imagine what millions of Jews in the U.S. and Israel could concoct.

The Holocaust Wars
What is Unique

- PGC believes that this second intellectual war is extremely important to win. By "win," PGC means:

  - At the least, the left leaning group of organizations will, <u>by necessity</u>, <u>drop the</u> Apartheid libel. If they can't, they should just worship it secretly. PGC will issue "the teaser" – not a "nice" one page attack to convey that this war will be "for keeps." <u>Israel is not an Apartheid state</u>; it is a safe haven that Jews never had for a very, very long time.
  In exchange for dropping this ugly libel, their opposing organizations will make some concessions (to be quietly negotiated).

- <u>Do you believe that Israel is an Apartheid state?</u>
- If so, consider the following Independence Day Parade. <u>Note Every Detail Carefully</u>.
  - The bearer of the Israeli flag is   a black as coal Ethiopian Jew
  - The marching first line consists of   a light brown as chocolate Yemeny Jew
                                                A lily white as clean linen Polish Jew
                                                A quite white Arab (oh, my God)

  - They are all reservists in IDF
    In their civilian life, they are all accomplished people

    The Black fellow, a reserve paratroop officer, owns a bookstore.
    The Brown man, a reserve officer in Golani, owns a construction company
    The White man, a reserve sergeant (he is still young) runs a tech company
    The White Arab, <u>a General</u> (oh, yes). He owns a farm.

  - By the way, the above will, as a colorful group, dine tonight at "Yellow Fellow" owned restaurant (this Vietnamese man was part of the "Boat People" Israel took in.)

  - If you believe the above, and you still call Israel an Apartheid State, YOU ARE INSANE!

  - If you don't believe the above, you are a misinformed, IRREDEEMABLE MEMBER (and a deplorable one) OF THE MARXIST'S "LUMPEN" (Not a nice word)

Jews have absorbed enough blood libels in 2000 year. Get it?

The Holocaust Wars
What is Unique
The Intellectual War

PGC believes that in some serious ways, the Holocaust is not over. This assertion is at the core of the third Holocaust war.

Some evidence is clearly presentable and convincing, some is obscure but is just as ominous.

The obvious evidence abounds.

The aggregate of resolutions by U.N. (in all its parts) multiple international organizations, internationally distributed media, distinguished academic institution and massive U.S. cultural institutions have never ceased and have increased attacks on Jews, Israel and any country that is Israel friendly (not many around …).

- For awhile, the gross attacks on Israel and Jews were simply assigned to Arab League substantial, well financed efforts. The MidEast, however, is undergoing a change with Israel establishing more relationships with Arab League States by the month. Thus, the source of growing **and that's a fact** attacks on Jews and on Israel must be assignable to other sources that impact this brazen increase.

1. PGC asserts that the source is coming from a new anti-U.S. realignment where the old, hundred-year sheriff, is tired of keeping aggressive Totalitarians at bay, the international security mechanisms aren't working, the U.S. Allies are contemplating their whiteness and climate change and get their military to develop their belies instead of fighting skills, corrupt Ivy League universities receive vast funds to help China steal our technology via Confucius centers.
2. How are anti-Israel and antisemitism connected to the above tirade? It is simple. If you want to show U.S. weakness, show how easy it is to have its top general deeply believe in his whiteness being dangerous and the danger to U.S. is

climate change. A weak U.S. is still strong to prevent Israel from taking down Iran's nuclear facilities.

When Iran becomes nuclear soon, so will the $ rich residents of the MidEast who'll buy the bomb from North Korea, the asylum state, or cash strapped Pakistan. This is just a small hint. More is covered in our Knowledge Base.

PGC's Knowledge Base contains data, information and intelligence re all the other Holocaust wars classifications, especially the potential physical wars in the near future. With that said, reality suggests that "A new/small company should only eat what it can chew! And thus, although PGC is not able to deal with all the issues that are beyond its competence, it is still necessary to point out that many a time, "The emperor is actually naked" and that PGC can, given the effort it already put in and the long experience in dealing with complexity, provide a decent platform to determine the Emperor's clothing status.

PGC has generated in multiple books, opinion pieces, white papers (essentially advocacy and propaganda) a reasonably consistent way at viewing the Holocaust <u>without worrying</u> about winning or losing government grants, endowments, corporate or lobbyists support.

Thus, <u>the Knowledge Base provides</u>:
- PGC's mission and objectives
- The various explanations, we promised, of events <u>and causality</u>
- Our view of an ugly world, we lived in and are still observing the same.
- Our view of the good, bad and ugly experts who run things
- Some humble and mild suggestion to deal with clear issues
- The website which provides the guidance to possible answers to non-TikTok questions (being WOKE is okay if you

are rational. We have no Holocaust dancing or musicals to suggest). We do have interesting spy and war fictional stories (not too farfetched …) which are admittedly propaganda pieces.

We relegate the above to separate books – now available. This introduction was aimed to just create an acquaintance with PGC.

I.5 THE HOLOCAUST WARS PROJECT

"THE QUESTIONS NOT ASKED AND THE ANSWERS NOT GIVEN"

An Opinion Piece

Presented by Project Gideon Company

("PGC")

To Be Shortly Launched

PGC EXPECTS THAT IT WILL GENERATE SEVERAL OPINION PIECES ON THE SAME TOPIC

THIS IS THE FIRST ENTRY.

WRITTEN BY: JACOB STERNBERG

PREFACE

- There seems to be a consensus, prevailing among historians and learned academics at large, that the Holocaust is the worst crime in history. The same consensus has led academics to conclude that <u>the crime is singular in all possible respects.</u>

- For the past EIGHT DECADES, thousands of institutions and a vast cadre of researchers have attempted – in the largest ever research project – to determine the facts and the causes for the Holocaust's occurrence.
  - <u>What</u> Happened?   • <u>How</u> Did It Happen?   • <u>Why</u> Did It Happen?

- As a result of the massive research effort, <u>much is known</u> (and much is verified) yielding near-infinite eyewitness testimony of the crimes committed against several categories of people defined by the Nazis as:
  - A specific race which poses an existential threat to the Aryan race and its
    empire of the future (The Jews)
  - Any persons who are "subhuman" (mentally and physically)
  - Any person with "aberrate behavior" (e.g., homosexuals, and Roma people)
  - A specific race which is naturally suited for hard work for the future Aryan
    empire (e.g., Slavs)

- The enormous data acquisition, verification/validation, data mining and making the data and information available and accessible to all, was much aided by the criminals themselves with an unusual fetish for keeping and preserving all data at all times and at all costs. Imagine how hard and costly it was without computers.

- We, at PGC – a company to be shortly launched – are dedicated to provide "Professionally-Generated" Holocaust Memorials "Intellectual Products" – to elevate memorials to respect not just the pain and suffering of the victims but provide the enormous heroics to be known and respected.

ROADMAP

Question 1 116

Question 2 117

Question 3 129

Question 4 136

Question 5 137

Aircraft Carrier Analogy 139

The Holocaust Wars
Questions
THE FIRST QUESTION

- Everybody knows ("Tom, Dick and Harry" especially) that the Centennial Memorial of the Holocaust will shortly occur. Assume that a logical choice would be 2035 being the 100th year of the Nuremberg Laws passage at the Reichstag. It is only 12 years to go.

    Question #1:   What will the Centennial Presentation consist of?

    True Answer: As of today (2023), nobody knows the answer exactly.

    Lame Answer: There is time. The closer we get to 2035, some reasonable suggestions will surface.

    Sub-Question

    (#1.1):   Who is the magician who will decide what to choose among some likely candidate ideas?

    Sub-Question

    (#1.2):   And when will that happen?

- A reasonably calm person, very knowledgeable, suggests to invite "Interested Parties" to a quiet retreat to deal with the Centennial Memorial issue.

    This is a good initial answer to Question #1.

    The poor soul, selected to handle Question #2 that follows, is so neutral to all the infighting among the very muscular and dedicated Jewish organizations that he poses no threat to anyone.

The Holocaust Wars
Questions
THE SECOND QUESTION

Question #2: What information do you need to know in order to provide a superior answer to Question #1?

True Partial Answer: As of today (2023), you <u>must know too many</u> very important information pieces. We first deal with <u>management issues</u>.

The reasons for knowing these information morsels is explained in many ways in the "Knowledge Base". A very sizeable collection on PGC books, opinion pieces, media coverage and plain ideas to achieve <u>insightful non-ad hoc presentations</u>	Determine the venues worldwide
	Determine the special political requirements for each venue (Israel, U.S., G. Britain, Poland, Germany, Lithuania, Argentina, France, Ukraine, Russia Denmark, Canada and others.)
	Determine the independence of the Centennial from international organizations
	Determine the participation of aggrieved non-Jewish peoples in the Centennial Memorials
	Establish a "<u>Jewish Medal of Honor</u>" with gradation proportional to risks taken by non-Jews.
	Establish a "Thank You Project."
	Establish a <u>working relationship with sponsors</u>
	Set up a media information distribution service
	Set up a robust security program for all Centennial memorials.
	Any glitch in any one venue will shift glitch-happy media to a wrong atmosphere for the seminal worldwide event.

On the day of PGC's debut, the Knowledge Base will be accessible to decision makers with interest in the Centennial Memorials.

- Besides the management information previously enumerated, extensive decisions are required regarding:

  - The mission and objectives of the presentations. Due to multiple venues and multiple sponsors, it is unlikely that a single format and a single products mix will suit all simultaneously presented memorials.

    In its suggested plans, PGC advises that:

    I. A minimal core presentation be professionally prepared.

    II. Locally-suited extensions and emphasis will likely not only improve the quality of the presentation but will allow proper "Thank You" clear messages and, simultaneously prevent some likely "Boo Boos." Examples will illustrate. (The Knowledge Base deals extensively with the above raised issues).

  - <u>The minimal core of a Holocaust presentation</u> is proposed to consist of the following "Products"

    I.1 A clear presentation of the crimes committed on the Jews – by virtue of <u>What was Done</u>.

    I.2 A clear presentation of the crimes committed on Jews and humanity – by virtue of <u>How it was Done</u>.

    I.3 A clear presentation of Nazi crimes by virtue of <u>Why it was Done</u> – and stays rather inexplicable to this day.

The Holocaust Wars
Questions

<u>The above constitutes The Pain and Suffering Portion of the Program</u>.

- ■ To augment the "Pain and Suffering" portion of the presentation requires additional minimal program segments:

    I.4   Clearly explain why the causality of the Holocaust ("Why did you do it?") is essential to minimize repetitions

    Clearly explain why, in spite of stellar institutions being populated by stellar researchers have not arrived at the "Why" answers yet.

    Incorporate the umbilical connection between Totalitarian/Deterministic cults and the atrocities/genocides for which the perps are the midwife

    I.5   Clearly explain why the seeming consensus view of the Holocaust does not incorporate the past (going back 2000 years) pogroms/atrocities/genocides directed at Jews specifically throughout the millennia (with some respite periods …)

    I.6   Clearly explain why, in the wake of World War II, Totalitarian cultish garbage (in the form of Soviet Kool Aid) <u>supported for 46 years</u> (1945-1991) <u>A Real World War III</u> (fought by surrogates) on every continent with dire consequences for many peoples/nations/tribes.

© Copyright The Project Gideon Company - 2023

The Holocaust Wars
Questions

I.7 Clearly explain that not all events are explicable. Some events are created by malignant perps whose actions, based on coagulated world views beyond human grasp. Consider the following:

I.7.1 "British troops were advancing on Neuengamme [A labor camp in northern Germany]

– Hitler has committed suicide a few days earlier [On April 30, 1945]

– SS Chief, Heinrich Himmler, has given orders not to surrender the camps with their prisoners.

– Guards put 8,000 inmates into two ships [Cap Arcona and Thielbeck]

– "On May 3, 1945, a British Air Force squadron, [knowing nothing about the ships' cargo] bombed and sank them."
Retracing a Lost Life
El Paso Times 12/18/2006

How malignant can a mind be to commit such an atrocity?

I.7.2 There exists no rational explanation for utterly dysfunctional international organizations that claim virtue and have none.

PGC provides numerous examples of the damages by the League of Nations and by the U.N. and other less than desirable international furuncles.

The Holocaust Wars
Questions

-They tolerate the existence of <u>an asylum state</u> (North Korea), brainless, cashless, foodless, member of the Nuclear Club which can cause Armageddon on a inflicted moment's notice. (just after its leader shot a hole in one on his first ever golfing appearance)

-Tolerate Iran – the most prolific terrorist state -<u>Ready to Achieve Nuclear Club Membership a</u>nd together with North Korea, create a nuclear bazaar.

<u>They Wish Armageddon to come</u> and Allah will provide the "Final Solution"

The Holocaust Wars
Questions

- To balance the Centennial Memorial "Pain and Suffering" presentation, it is necessary to present the following segments:

I.8.1 The heroics involved in numerous ghetto uprisings and the heroics of <u>a vast array of non-Jews</u> whose deeds cover the spectrum from

— Titanic efforts, including real major physical fights

— Enormous risk taking by hiding Jews

— A huge number of inventive meaningful resistance(e.g., the strain of typhus invented by two Polish doctors which actually panicked the Nazis and enabled effective resistance

— A huge number of quietly getting food and clothing to the destitute peoples

It is imperative to introduce into the Holocaust Memorial the true notions that:

I.8.2 The Nazis weren't what they are popularly perceived to be.

They actually <u>proved to be military idiots</u>. Adam Tooze shows how they fought on four fronts simultaneously with huge resources eaten up by the "Jewish Front." (A costly 4th front) – All in severe shortage of fuel, steel, chemicals and vast shortages of productive labor.

The Holocaust Wars
Questions

> The SS weren't the dimwits hooligans who obeyed loudly barked orders. PGC sites data pointing to 25% of SS had Ph.D.'s and numerous psychiatric and eugenics geniuses who wanted to help nature to cull sub humans (all for improving mankind's chances to survive and live better lives …)

I.8.3 The vaunted German industrial sector that chose to employ underfed, badly treated, sick demoralized and terrorized workers, proved to be no better than their military.

> PGC contrasts the use of slave labor by the German industrial geniuses with the U.S. response to labor shortages. Good looking, smart, productive "Rosie the Riveter" not only produced products, she could fly the planes to embarkation depots to save Europe's bacon.

II. Given the availability of the minimal set of standard professionally prepared segments, we turn to Desirable, Location-Specific Segments, to Improve Receptibility by Audiences.

Although PGC has limited capabilities in this area, it does analyze in several opinion pieces (part of PGC's Knowledge Base) which advocate some logical segments.

II.1 Local Appendages to Standard Products.

II.1.1 It is likely that the Memorial in Germany will be in Nuremberg – the city that gave us all the "Nuremberg Laws" (quite obnoxious). PGC believes that the "Mark of Cain" that has sullied the German people for a long time, must at some point disappear.

Only an incredible event can achieve that. At a minimum, <u>a professionally prepared</u> "Never Again" segment might be helpful to the "Get Out of Jail" card. PGC is not well suited to provide any final suggestions.

The decades long German effort, when adequately presented, providing "Mea Maxima Culpa" and an unequivocal commitment of "Never Again," should work.

II.1.2 It is likely that the Memorial in Poland will occur in Warsaw – the city that provided us all with a heroic uprising.

Poland believes that it has been subjected to what it characterizes as a bum rap re its treatment of Polish Jews both historically and in the 20th Century specifically.

Poland is a proud country. It resisted Soviet dominance with great courage. It had robust partisan groups giving the Nazis a hard time. Right at the start of WWII, the Nazis decimated the Polish Intelligencia. Polish resistance secured the stealing of the enigma which played a major role in allied intelligence operation.

| Whatever they say it better be professionally prepared. | Numerous Poles have been recognized as major heroes by receiving from Israel the equivalent of the "Jewish Medal of Honor." |

With all the truly laudable thoughts above, it is true that:

| It is not for nothing that the Nazis have created multiple camps in a land that they thought could actually tolerate them. | Poland had experienced major pogroms just after VE Day (May 8, 1945) in many of its cities. |

The author of this paper was a "7-year-old journalist" witnessing a Wroclaw pogrom.

REMEMBER: Jewish Blood of WWII has not yet clotted.

The Holocaust Wars
Questions

Some Polish powerful idiots wanted to have a meat production factory in one of the many camps. Imagine the intellectual crime!

"No Ticky -- No Shirty"   To get a "Get Out of Jail" card, Poland will have to produce an exemplary "Mea Maxima Culpa" and mean it.

II.1.3 It is not just Germany and Poland that need a "Get Out of Jail" card.

PGC is suggesting that Ukraine, Belarus, Argentina, France and others could benefit if their Holocaust Memorials contain some well-meant Mea Culpa knowing that it is important to handle specific transgressions that are far in excess of just minor forgivable events.

Ukraine has had a long antisemitic history. Later, in 1919, it had what may be labeled as a "mini-Holocaust."

Argentina has accepted Dr. Mengele and Eichmann as legitimate refugees – these perps are Satan's offspring

II.1.4 Some tailor-made appendages for local presentations should be highlighted. Specifically:

Denmark, as a country, did all the right things. It moved most of "its Jews" to neutral Sweden. Its Red Cross made exceptional efforts that the "Potemkin Village Concentration Camp" (Theresienstadt) treat its citizens and its young inmates more humanely.

It is quite rational to give that entire country a "Medal of Honor" and state why!

The same thought should be allocated to the United States of America for its clobbering the monsters.

PGC covers much more ground. We have specific suggestions for specific themes for specific countries.

The Holocaust Wars
Questions
THE THIRD QUESTION

Question #3: What makes you confident that a small startup company can achieve the mission as stated?

True Answer: If "Success" is <u>REALISTICALLY</u> and <u>PRACTICALLY</u> defined, a predefined minimal level of success can <u>AND MUST</u> be achieved

- The Following Guides PGC "Realism":

  Clear understanding that a "Pain and Suffering" message will be balanced by a clear "Heroics and Defiance" message.

  – There are numerous ways of delivering an insightful "Pain and Suffering" story as a centerpiece for all the simultaneously presented events.

  – The chosen centerpiece will be augmented with specific appendages suitable to the different audiences in the multiple presentation venues.

  – The same is true for the "Heroics and Defiance" segment.

  Not bickering about the above requires a high degree of diplomatic skills.

  PGC proposes a number of examples to avoid the urges of extracting the last tear, nor a false 007 heroics.

  We expect that the examples will illuminate this aspect.

© Copyright The Project Gideon Company - 2023

- A clear understanding that the Centennial Holocaust events do not constitute some Oscar-competitive artistic events for entertainment.

  – Face it, people, nothing in the "Information Age" escapes the urge to present propaganda films, documentaries, dignitaries/celebrities' speeches, live or recorded, Tik Tok influencers (who sing or dance) or customary (in the not too recent past) Soviet yearly festivals for the youth of the world "solidarity" events.

  – The events we advocate also reflect our urge to deliver clear messages. And these messages are not complicated.

  Historically, millennia ago, major empires jousted to get prisoners and booty to display in victorious parades when coming home.

  About a thousand years ago, major empires jousted to prove religious superiority of their God.

  Hundreds of years ago, major empires jousted to acquire colonies and slaves to enrich the winners.

The Holocaust Wars
Questions

"History is a foreign country, THEY DID IT DIFFERENTLY THERE"   (Hartley, a British writer)

In those days, one could surrender or religiously convert and survive.

The survival choice was taken away from the Jews. They weren't just "killed," they were "EXTERMINATED" with terror, humiliation, pain and deceit, all meticulously planned.

The Holocaust Wars
Questions

We know that Holocausts don't just happen. Pogroms, atrocities and genocides (including very large-scale ones) happened all over the world and quite frequently. <u>NOTHING LIKE THE HOLOCAUST HAS HAPPENED EXCEPT ONCE.</u>

We have the urge, unstoppable, no matter how hard to realize, to tell:

NEVER AGAIN, NOT NOW, NOT LATER, NOT EVER!

Our urge to tell is anchored in very solid ground.

PGC spared no effort in dissecting the term singular in describing the dementia, malignancy ultimate cruelty and other Satanic "Qualities" of the perpetrators.

PGC <u>umbilically connects Totalitarian cults as the sole midwives of the Holocaust</u>. No one can even conceive what these bastards did.

PGC <u>connects the cumulatively created blood libels</u> directed at Jews to an unstoppable sequence of atrocities over two millennia.

The wake of the Holocaust created a highly skilled imitator of atrocities against numerous tribes/nations/countries and cultures who promised a Garden of Eden Utopian Future which took 46 years to defeat (1945-1991). The "Kool Aid" was and is powerful enough to bring in even a newer wannabe "Holocauster," the one that locks exits from big buildings for people who want to leave the buildings because of the ultimate police state "Diktat." Think of Covid and China.

PGC makes a special effort to deal with the disoriented Jews who, by surviving, became subjects of pity, "Driftwoods of WWII," PTSD'd and many who still cannot overcome victimology.

It is for these people that a vast effort is necessary to stress the Jewish heroics of resistance and physical actual war heroics.

PGC strongly believes that non-Jewish heroics were <u>EXHIBITED BY MILLIONS OF NON-JEWS</u>, and we point to real data, consider just samples.

- ***   Entire Countries (Denmark) – Resistance

- ***   Entire Countries (U.S.A.) – Physical <u>Annihilators</u> of the swine and Economic Recovery

In PGC's view, Anti-U.S. sentiments have dug up here and there about "U.S. not doing enough" …

<u>**COMPARED TO WHOM? – ANSWER THE QUESTION!**</u>

- *** Non-Jewish Titans of resistance of stellar character

    Diplomats (Wallenberg, et al)

    Doctors (Polish duo who spooked German authorities with a typhus strain and numerous others)

    Churches and social workers **(we especially like Irena)**

    Numerous partisan groups

    And never forget Leski, PGC likes him a lot …

- *** Non-Jewish giants of resistance of the "rogue" variety. e.g. Schindler, Skorzeny and others

- *** Non-Jewish "Simple Folk" who hid, fed and kept silent

GOD BLESS YOU ALL!!!

THE HOLOCAUST WARS PROJECT

"THE QUESTIONS NOT ASKED AND THE ANSWERS NOT GIVEN"

An Opinion Piece

THIS IS THE SECOND ENTRY

WRITTEN BY: JACOB STERNBERG

THE FOURTH QUESTION

Question #4: Given the importance you assign to PGC's mission, the seminal nature of the Holocaust events and the likely interest by multiple political entities, the likely loud noise of real and not so real conflicts and given too many management issues to handle,

HOW WILL YOU RANK YOUR SUGGESTED EVENTS' CHANCES OF SUCCESS?

True Answer: Put on the tight shoes

- Accept the reality that there will be a small chance to generate a "minimal success" (not difficult to define)
- Fight like Hell for key small achievements
- Take the tight shoes off for a bit
- Make sure that the Jewish kids have guts/honor/Kool Aid avoidance **powered by a robust education program.**
- Much more is provided in PGC's suggested plans.

To avoid doubt that a "Minimal Success" is achievable, PGC has generated a comprehensive proposed example of the entire Centennial presentation in Washington, D.C. on May 15, 2035 combining 100th year of Nuremberg Laws disaster nearly 2000 years to the rebirth of a Jewish country destroyed in 70 C.E.

Oh, what a comeback!

This plan is presented in this separate attachment.

THE FIFTH QUESTION

Question #5: Avoiding too many general descriptions, too many explanations/justifications

What is it exactly that you propose for a Washington, D.C., Centennial Memorial on <u>May 15, 2035</u>?

Answer:
- Buckle Up!

- Remember, "We Have the Meats – but we never made

  sandwiches before"

- We have time to practice

  And we know who are good "Sandwich Makers"

  And they are expensive

- You will be presented with a <u>Detailed Rough Draft</u> and <u>We are Humble Enough</u> and we <u>Have the Chutzpa</u> to talk back. There is no limit to our love of Israel, our adoration for the U.S. and our disdain for Totalitarians (the midwives of atrocities).

Although, in our careers, we have never had technological failures (EVER!) we know how to err in other components of projects implementation – too many to recite …

For us, "The Holocaust Wars Project" is a calling, an honor and we have skin in this. Hence, the promise of dedication of experienced implementors of promises they make.

Here We Come.

To shorten our presentations and to make things clearer, we present brief tutorial analogies.

The Aircraft Carrier Analogy

- To project power, U.S. has Aircraft Carriers.

    They can sustain operations for a long time

    They are an Air Force base (many planes) with an airport wherever they locate

    They have essential services (feed 5,000 people a day three meals, have power for all functions, have desalinated water, a hospital, an entertainment center, have multiple communications and weaponry for a real fight – and many other functions)

    > In an emergency, they can supply power to even Vladivostok!!

    Among their weaknesses are the need to protect it from a gang of enemy submarines, frequent resupplies, sad crews who need sometimes to come home and a host of support frigates, destroyers and probably a host of other things we forgot to mention.

    We will refer to such carrier as a "Flagship."

We will, by analogy to this "Flagship," refer to some films, books, plays or opinion pieces with an appended "Flagship." For instance, Lucas produced the first StarWars movie as a flagship film. It provided the political/cultural background for a future organized world structure. It introduced all the main characters, the primary relationship among them, the main moral precepts at play, it identified the wide variety of views, strengths, weaknesses and above all, it was, First and Foremost, interesting. But it gave us more: You could easily link new episodes to this flagship without repeating details previously introduced and thus create new films that expanded the meaning of "interesting."

The Holocaust Wars
Questions

- The Holocaust is a set of events that occurred only once because it is singular/unique from any conceivable angle.

Rich Brownstein, a stellar researcher at Yad Vashem has identified about 400 Holocaust movies of which he judged "as worthy" about 50 of them.

Interestingly, it confirms to this very learned fellow that this "worthy" designation aligns the huge films industry output ratio of 11% of films that are "worthy."

It is obvious to him and to any expert that there isn't a one flagship film covering all of the Holocaust facts, views, crimes and perps.

And yet, a flagship film is required, even if it covers only a fraction of what you want to say.

The example we picked is simple, understandable, not pretentious. It will <u>introduce</u> the viewer and <u>connect</u> the viewer to the key events and world views that govern the Holocaust.

This flagship film manuscript has been written in parts.

(Nobody in our shop has the "Golden Touch" to stitch these meats into sandwiches)

We now lead you patiently through the parts.

The Holocaust Wars
Questions

PART ONE ("Place and Time")

- <u>Mendl Goldfarb</u> (Mendl is a Jewish name, Goldfarb is German, and Yiddish "Gold Color") <u>is born in Chelm, Poland</u> (Close to the Ukrainian border) on June 16, 1930.

Mendl is a fictional character.

Chelm is a real Polish town.

- A Jewish visitor from Palestine ("Moshe," a fictional character) in a scene at dinner in the Goldfarb home. It is Mendl's 8th birthday.

- The father of Mendl, Yehuda, explains to the curious visitor all about Chelm. Yehuda and his entire family are fictional.

- Yehuda provides <u>Real Facts and Some Fictional Data</u>.

The town exists for hundreds of years, it is about 50:50 populated by Jews. Total population about 60,000. ("It is what we call a shtetl") –

Jews occupy trading jobs, they produce shoes and clothing items, they work hard – many work 12-hour days. "It is a poor town, hard to feed many children, live in non-stone homes which many times burn down. The sanitary conditions are appalling. "We, thank God, are well to do. We have a stone home. We also have the ability and honor to have you as a guest and discuss important things."

The Goldfarb family home is shown as a well structured and furnished home. The dinner is served by Mendl's mother, Leah, and daughter, Dina, and, of course, a young maid. All food served look appetizing and appealing. The women join the dinner table, a sign of progressivity.

Small talk at the dinner table discloses the fictional "Facts" that Mendl, unlike his older two brothers, is very good in all the cheder studies, speaks Hebrew well and, of all things, is a very fine chess player. Moshe is impressed and suggests some chess for next day.

The scene shifts to a fine appointed room, Yehuda and Moshe sit down for a meeting that Yehuda arranged months earlier.

Yehuda displays knowledge and understanding of what the <u>Real Facts</u> prevail in the terrible world. He recited to his guest his concerns about March 13 of <u>this year</u> of the Anschluss of Austria, coincided (within days) with German bombing of Barcelona in Spain's Civil War, the Italians' bombing Guernica in Spain's Basque country last year and a host of other German aggressiveness vis-à-vis Czechoslovakia and Poland and his dark thoughts about aggression against the Jews everywhere.

Yehuda further mentioned in his recital of concerns for the Jews in Palestine surrounded by vastly outnumbered and Nazi sympathetic leadership of the Mufti in Jerusalem.

Yehuda intimated that shtetl like Chelm, thought of by Jews and Goyim as a town of Funny Fools is, <u>in fact</u>, having <u>five Yiddish newspapers for no more than 15,000 adults</u> has unusually active Kehilla activities of social services (helping the poor, medical clinics, extensive Jewish and secular education) and political activities, even sports teams. Yehuda himself has always been a Zionist. He was wondering whether he should pack up his family and get to Palestine.

The Holocaust Wars
Questions

He contacted some friends in Warsaw and they suggested to get a "Shalyach" (a messenger) from Palestine to mull it over. The underlying assumption by all was that Yehuda was able to finance the Kumzits ("come/sit"). Yehuda implemented the idea.

Up to this point, the film's story attempts to achieve the following messages:

1. Chelm could be considered a <u>Typical Jewish Shtetl</u>

2. Independent of reputation (e.g., Funny Fools), it had an active Jewish traditional social life while, generally, Chelm was a town of poor and hard-working Jews.

3. *Who, in his right mind, could want to annihilate these people?*

The film highlighted so far, the key background ideas that the world is engulfed in some atmospheric turbulence into which key characters are thrown in. We start with the film's hero.

<u>Mendl, now 8 years</u> old, he is introduced for several reasons.

1. He was born an usually bright child with all the typical signals of brilliance – early age speech, sense of humor and some hints of planned mischief, highly educable and capable communicator.

The Holocaust Wars
Questions

In this fictional film, we prefer to introduce him, almost as a symbol for his entire shtetl (considered, erroneously, as funny fools) by the following devices:

(1.) He has devastatingly sharp humor

(2.) He mastered chess quite early in life

(3.) He grasps the benefits of diplomacy – he will need it to survive

To illustrate his humor, the following short scene is presented:

His sister, Dina, cleans after dinner dishes at the kitchen sink. She loudly calls Mendl, who is not far away, but pretends not to hear her loud calling. He very slowly moves closer to her and with a fiendish smile asks whether anything wrong justifies her screaming. "Bring me the cleaning agent" – she says. She uses a highbrow expression. He slowly moves away. The sister is now exasperated by what she sees. Mendl holds the hand of the maid and seems to drag the maid to the sink. He smiles and utters "You asked for it" and adds: "Next time, ask for soap."

- To illustrate his active mind, even in his early years, we show Mendl play with a whole bunch of kids, a game they concocted called war. Boys like these games. It is real to the kids. They thought and made up rules re prisoner capture and treatment, what constitutes a win, how to execute diversions and a host of very silly other rules. All this to show how they fare in arguing disputes. No dirty words were used but "idiot" and choice Russian curses were dominant.

    Who, in his right mind, could want to annihilate these people?

- A new boy, an apparent visitor from a neighboring shtetl, asks Mendl whether the Chelm-born gang has yet captured the moon as it is to so known in the entire country. "The reason you dumb people think that we Chelmers did it is because you thought that we captured the moon's silhouette in the water barrel, covered the barrel and called it a "capture." All your friends, the geniuses, thought much about it and took the cover off the barrel and let the moon escape from the water barrel. After all, you geniuses are over seven years old and you can all already walk and capture
moons. "Only in Poland!" he added.

- There are added scenes that illustrate Mendl's intellectual prowess. On the day of Moshe's stay with Goldfarb household, Mendl suggested a game of chess. Mendl informed Moshe, smilingly, that he is a good player even though he is quite young. The game was set. Mendl won the first game on the strength of a well-executed attack. The older fellow suggested a rematch. At this game, Mendl adopted defense. Mendl won, this time on the strength of his defense and threats of counterattack.

The Holocaust Wars
Questions

Mendl noticed Moshe's difficulty after the second loss. He decided to propose a third game. This time, he decided to get a loss. As he later described to his father, the loss was intentional. To achieve the loss without committing silly errors, Mendl needed a good looking attack that, many moves later, will fizzle and lead to Mendl's loss. The kid realized that Moshe's ego was hurt after two successive losses and he planned an attack that must fail. Mendl recognized that Moshe will (a) Be happy to win (b) He won't realize that the plan was sufficiently long range and would not be considered to occur as just an error – and this was the hard part.

- Thus, a diplomat was born in Chelm.

[Many years later, Mendl remembered how he honed in his diplomatic skills. It all started with a terrible libel against Poland. Everybody knows that many national groups somehow believe that some other nationals are stupid. Norwegians and Swedes have thought that of each other. Canadians think that Ukrainians are stupid. Many national groups somehow clung to the notion that Poles are stupid.

To buttress this libelous idea, numerous supporting stories were invented and widely distributed. The first and more benign story was Mendl's favorite when he was young. It runs as follows: A math competition in Warsaw for kids under ten was in full swing. A major venue, seating 2,000 eager supporters of the contestant, has seated on the stage a moderator, three judges and ten contestants. Within 60 minutes each contestant has been asked and answered questions and those who failed to provide the right answer were eliminated and the others went to the next round.

Finally, two contestants remained. Stanislav and Yashek remained. Stanislav just failed a question and the sole remaining contestant (Yashek) was told that should he correctly answer the question, he will be the champion. The question: "$X^3 = 64$. What is the value of X?" Yashek has ten seconds. He thinks deeply, looks around. Ten seconds is a long time. The crowd is noisy. The bell rings and Yashek says "X = 4." The moderator turns to the judges to check the correctness. The crowd yells in unison: "Give him another chance, give him another chance." There were multiple ways to end this story:

1. After the chants by the public, crowds were eliminated by EU rules from all future math competitions east of France.

2. The EU constitution was amended to provide more time to answer math questions <u>and</u> allowing a contestant to have one refusal in the competition which he/she feels is "unfair" (compared to other contestants' questions or uneasy about going to the bathroom)]

- Mendl remembered another Polish tale in the libels category. This one differed from all other libels re Poland. Mendl made it all up, certainly the ending at least.

  A post-WWII Polish prime minister decided that Poland has suffered enough from the libel that Poles are stupid. He calls the entire Academy of Sciences to a nice retreat and tells them that the Polish best and brightest should execute a project to once and for all will be the burial for all anti-Polish libelous views of stupidity.

  The members assemble, are subjected to serious exhortations, they deeply analyze multiple suggestions. They settle on a favorite one and notify the prime minister the timing, the budget and request his approval.

The Holocaust Wars
Questions

>The prime minister approves the project. He doesn't even ask what it is.

- They come back a year later. The spokesman proudly presents the picture of the world's longest bridge. It is actually gorgeous looking.

    >"Where was this bridge placed?" he asked.

    >"In the Sahara Desert" came the answer.

    >The prime minister goes blue and livid. "You idiots placed this bridge in the Sahara Desert?"

    >"But we did it in one year. It was never done before!"

    >The prime minister feels sick. He barely lets out:
    >>"Go back and destroy it before everybody grasps how stupid we really are."
    >
    >Feeling very sick, he vomits and runs out of the meeting.

    >It is not over yet! Stay with us.

- A week later, the team charged with destroying the bridge has returned to see the prime minister.

    >"Have you destroyed it?" he asks.

    >"No, we couldn't," they answered.

    >"Why couldn't you, idiots?" he asks.

    >"We couldn't because the members of the entire U.N. General Assembly stood on the bridge fishing," they answered.

    >"You idiots, there are no fish in that desert!" he screamed.

    >"We all know that. But, the General Assembly has congratulated us for providing an iconic structure that symbolizes that overfishing will make the bridge in the desert a monument to remind us all of overuse of resources. We have been declared 'heroes.'"

    >The Prime minister went to church and prayed for them all. He also stopped fishing.

The second part of this "Flagship Film" starts with actual war scenes. The war scenes are viewed from Mendl's vantage point. He tells a doctor in the Warsaw Hospital, where he was brought after the first bombing of Warsaw. He got a concussion and was treated by a Jewish doctor. Bandages help in stopping the bleeding in his cheek. "Kid, we will help you to get out of here. This is Olga, she is a nun and she will get you out of here. Where is your family?" Mendl could not answer, it was all blurry. He could not remember what happened to them after a bomb exploded and demolished the building they were in.

- A scene is shown where Mendl is in a farmhouse on the outskirts of a forest. It was night. The nun who brought him to the farm told Mendl that he should stay there for a while until he gets better. She will come for him and see what needs to be done next. The farmers, two teenage boys, befriended Mendl. The nun told him to be "Yashek," not Mendl, and he understood.

- The farm boys liked their newly found small friend. The kid knew so much. He explained to them how airplanes fly and they were fascinated. They watched German planes who flew at high altitude. Mendl recouped, was picked up by the nun who took him to a hastily built small camp in the forest and left him there in the care of a big man who seemed to Mendl to be the commander.

  He was now nine years old. He was told that his job would entail to frequently get to the farm and bring some pig fat, salt and other small packages from the farm. His farm boys' friends will wait for him at appointed time.

  > "Can you read the clock time if I give you this pocket watch?"
  > Mendl answered affirmatively.
  > "Are you afraid to be lost?"
  > "No," answered Mendl (now responding to Yashek)

- Mendl quickly grasped that the little camp in the forest was a partisans' "home." The men would depart most nights for some missions having to do with the ongoing war.

  Mendl became curious and followed a group of men on their mission. He was happy to see the teenage farm boys in that group. When the boys recognized Yashek, they warned him to tag along at a distance. He was too small to participate in their war. Yashek knew to listen to good advice.

  In the few months he spent with the partisans, he listened to their discussions, to briefings by their commander and realized, all at once, that he needs to change things. He didn't know what. He knew that he needs to get to Byalistok. The Russians and the Germans weren't fighting. The commander told him that he, Yashek, the little "Jewish pig" will fare better on the Russian side and maybe have a chance to be something better than an errand boy.

- Mendl would up on the Russian border just before mid-1941. Mendl was now eleven years old, quite hardened by the last two years' experiences. The border guards examined him thoroughly. He had no documents, his story was not detailed, his clothes were mended multiple times, he looked tired and yet he had a very intelligent speech. They asked how he had survived in German occupied territory, they asked this youngster about his family, he truthfully answered that he had no idea what happened to them after the bombing. The guards found the boy interesting. He, even in his condition, answered some questions with humor. All he wanted, he said, was to go to school. He loves to learn things. They gave him displaced person papers and directed him to a group that handled young orphans. He wound up in an orphanage in the City of Tomsk, in Siberia.

The Holocaust Wars
Questions

- There are clear breaks in this Flagship Film in the way it was presented so far. This was done on purpose. This version of the film will be shown to preteens and they need to be shown only what they can bear without nightmares.

  [A substitute segment with all the blood and gore will be available when shown to middle to late teenagers and adult audiences.

  The period end of 1939 to end of 1941 was devoted by the Nazis to prepare for massive "Industrial Strength" exterminations of Jews and live testing of extermination methods. We omit describing it here in detail, we will just hint:

  - First, the Nazis went after the Polish Intelligencia

  - Second, rough calculations of extermination per day in the end '39 to end '41 period resulted in less than 200 Jews exterminated per day. When 1942 kicked in, the number of Jews exterminated per day rose to near 5,000. This vast difference will be shown and its Satanic implications highlighted.

  - The Nazis introduced humiliations, terror and deception to reduce any urge to resist to their well-practiced methods in all stages of the extermination process.

    And all of it will be told as close to reality as possible.]

  It is important to introduce, via the Flagship Film, the notion that the Nazis weren't the only Totalitarian cult capable of inflicting mega atrocities.

The Holocaust Wars
Questions

- The likely name of the Flagship Film is "The Holocaust Wars"

  One segment will be devoted to Mendl's story while in Russia beginning in mid-1941. This segment does require alternates for simple and obvious reasons.

  - For educational programs for the young, Mendl's story at the orphanage can be unpleasant enough but cannot dwell on barbaric treatment. Hints of cruelty will suffice.

    Mendl suffered enough in the suddenness of loss of family, making it through two years on his wits at ages 9, 10 and then being in a Russian orphanage.

    For the young viewers, the stress will be showing scenes where Mendl covers up his tremendous intelligence. Standouts do not do well in such places.

    For regular showing at Holocaust Memorials, it is important to show the Mendl smarts and character – "A good exhibit of character is always smart defiance of evil."

    The theme of defiance must permeate the entire film.

  - Mendl's stay in Russia should deliver additional "messages" to adult audiences.

    Current audiences have ambivalent attitudes toward Russia in its multiple incarnations in the past 100+ years. Pre-revolutionary Russia was essentially a vast continent size patched together tribal lands, run by despots forever engaged in central and eastern regions wars of different sizes.

The 1917 Revolution, a result of an extreme Totalitarian deterministic cults effort with exceptionally strong Avant Garde cadre cobbled together a powerful country.

Russia preceded the Fascist Totalitarian empire dream by constantly feeding its population which never tasted freedom tremendous Kool Aid dosages, fighting off Western attempts to intervene and projecting a strong influence in Western countries affairs.

A film segment will show that in spite the orphanage's brutality of the staff, Mendl's "cloaking" (or masking) his innate intelligence to avoid being a standout and a target for bullies, and the generally poverty-level provisions of food, clothing, education, involvement in sports and culture, the tireless KGB worked everywhere and they recognized that they have a tasty morsel in all the chaff.

A married Jewish couple, both physicians in Tomsk, were desperate to adopt a child and kept visiting the orphanage. The local quite wise KGB man "helped" to direct their attention to Mendl – "A nice Jewish boy." The couple fell in love with the boy. Mendl Goldfarb was adopted by the Goldshtein couple.

- The reader is aware that the plot is fictional. With that said, this segment tells facts about Minsk, the new parents, and concocts a story that is highly believable and, when later, other film segments, or entire films will be plugged in, not much "explaining" will be needed. Pay attention to Tomsk and the KGB.

- Tomsk is a Siberian city which I know rather well. I spent nearly seven years (1993-2000), 50% of my time in Russia and much of it in Siberia. (I tell this real-life story in my memoir – "Jacob's Odyssey" – a part of this project's Knowledge Base)

The Holocaust Wars
Questions

- ▲ Russia was not all "Potemkin Village" mirages. Tomsk had stellar learning/research institutes populated by exiles from teeming Moscow and St. Petersburg (later Leningrad) environments. Smart talents builds smart institutions.

- ▲ To help the population consume the party's sizeable Kool Aid servings, they had powerful (intellectually and physically endowed) state servants whose training of agents was superb and accomplishments plentiful in both Russia and many countries abroad.

  By stressing the above, we pave the way for future segments where Mendl (later Vadim Molotov) performs some services for Mother Russia.

- ▲ In the field of atrocities, Russia occupies a strange place. It has an incredibly honorable position due to its heroic contribution to the defeat of the abominable Third Reich.

  It also holds a most dishonorable position in all of history by subjugating a vast number of countries, suppressing freedoms of all important thoughts and deed, directly causing (through surrogates) ongoing wars and massacres on all continents and effectively participating in World War Three (1945-1991).

  The Soviet Union, unlike the Nazis, learned to "cloak" its misdeeds in very clever ways.

I.6   THE RANCHER'S RANT

I.6 THE RANCHER'S RANT
AN OPINION PIECE FROM THE MANUSCRIPT
"TROLLERS' WARS" (Formatted as a Play)

"I have a message to all America Haters:
Remember, the U.S. does 'good' and does it 'well,'
and, at the end of the day, U.S. wins.
It did in WWI, WWII and WWIII.
WWIV is special. I am here to tell you a bit about it.

(Theodor H. Troller III (TTIII) The Rancher)

"Also remember that the foot you stepped on today
is connected to the derrière you might have to kiss tomorrow."
(TTIII)

The Holocaust Wars
Rancher's Rant
<u>Act III. Scene 1</u>

[The stage lights up. A newcomer walks toward the table seating the Troller offsprings.]

<u>NARRATOR</u>: The newcomer is Theodor H. Troller III ("TTIII"). [TTIII stands up. He has an uncanny resemblance to the Marlboro man appearing on numerous billboards in the U.S.]

<u>TTIII</u>: I am the last male in Theodor H. Troller sequence. All my kids are girls.

It is not easy to be in this bloodline. I am not a medical doctor as my grandfather TTI was, I am not a prolific inventor/scientist as my father TTII was. I am, plain and simple, a rancher – I look like one, talk like one, behave like one and hold the beliefs of a rancher. As part of it, I naturally mock city slickers on both U.S. coasts who pretend to be sophisticated, all knowing, all caring and, in short, "love humanity but hate people" who are "deplorable and irredeemable," just like me.

I have been listening to you all yapping about my father, TTII. Chrissy here (many a time I call her Crusty as befitting a tough little woman helping build nuclear bombs and a nuclear navy), keeps yapping about our father's sins. I don't know enough about Marx, Freud, Harvard Law, International law, history of many nations, persecution of Jews throughout history and a whole array of sins of white men, imperialists, dirty capitalists, European pretenders to be diplomatic geniuses. But I do know a few important things, and those I hold dear.

1. I don't think TTII, my father, is guilty of anything. Look here, Crusty, Jacob has told you many times and worked hard to convince you that "if you were in father's shoes, you wouldn't want to be Jewish. Would you want your daughter to be one? Period.

2. It is no secret that father was involved in two World Wars, the second and third. He was terrific at the second and it seemed that he did very little for the third. But that is not true. His work on security systems prior to and during WWII were of extremely significant value. Let's all stand up and salute the old coot. The third World War required aerodynamic innovations that eventually led to the Soviet demise because of their inability to compete. Salute again.

3. I know for a fact that when nearly the entire world worshipped the Soviet Union in the 1950's, all the way to USSR's demise in 1991, he taught us kids about the totalitarian regimes misdeeds. He told whoever will listen about the Soviet's vulnerabilities and drew whatever little optimism he could gather from it.
<u>He knew</u> that they can't compete with us in space, in spite of the Sputnik episode. If the U.S. could take away from them the first strike capability, <u>EVEN A DUMB RANCHER LIKE ME KNOWS THAT THEY CAN'T WIN</u>.

4. I learned from him to respect what facts tell you and disrespect mostly empty slogans.

I have lived on this ranch nearly all my life. Since 1952, that's 67 years. I'm a real environmentalist. I seriously conserve water. I let my cattle graze on the land. This is a big ranch and can support grazing for many heads of cattle. I have had chickens and sheep and, years ago, I had peach orchards. I had all animals treated humanely. There is a mountain lion on the mountain on my land; we don't bother him and he leaves us alone.

My ranch is a gorgeous place. It is a mile high; it has beautiful views of the Chirakawa mountain range and a fascinating mountain façade called Cathedral Rock.

On my ranch there is a small stream – really small – which has, in some years, not all, some water running. Water, as you all know, is a rare commodity in these lands here. On occasion, I would like to dam the damned thing with just a few rocks and use the water. But I can't. The regulators forbid it.

<u>Regulators love to regulate</u>, and they are convinced that they are right all the time. I am fortunate that they didn't call it a 'navigable river." Wait a bit, they may yet do it.

Many years ago, I read in Playboy magazine that in Minnesota you cannot walk backwards on Sundays. As I said, regulators love to regulate. I don't know if this regulation is still on the books there. I haven't read Playboy in decades.

- One day the peach trees got a nasty disease. There was nothing we could do but cut the trees. Sad day. I remember how tasty those peaches were.

I am compelled to tell you all <u>that nature could and actually is a bitch</u>. On the one hand, it produces unimaginably beautiful vistas, provides incredibly colorful flowers which also smell good, it provides a vast number of nutrients and – you get the drift…And then on the other hand, it also fosters incredibly fierce bacteriological and chemical warfare in the plant world – it is unceasing warfare over territory.

In the animal world, a well-structured food chain discloses the permanent ongoing killing and mercilessly devouring their prey. In the non-human segment of the animal world, the interspecies warfare is not limited to food alone. It covers, surprisingly, territorial hegemony and in some cases just plain hate (lions hate hyenas …).

The human segment has elevated "the permanent nature of within-species warfare" to ideologically infected cruelty.

Nature actually engages in a permanent war against all living things – volcanic eruptions, tsunamis, hurricanes, tornados, floods, fires – all contribute to brutal/cruel outcomes. To make it worse, Mother Nature will produce earthquake aftershocks if it deems that the main eruption didn't do enough damage."

Before you get all depressed, I want to convey to you some simple cowboy wisdom.

1. You all know Isiah who fervently believed and conveyed the message that "in the end of days" the lion and the sheep will cease the predator and prey relationship. This kills the notion of the cruelty of the food chain relationship.

2. The assertions that warfare, permanent or not, is a "bad state" because it causes suffering, death and destruction, does not take into account that improvements and renewals require some elimination of old to allow the new and possibly the better to prevail.
3. When the biblical Job vehemently complains to God about being unjustly subjected to punishments he didn't deserve, Job gets his comeuppance by being unequivocally told that he has no idea about the enormity of the power he derides, he should stop complaining. Job did. A further interesting outcome occurred. His wealth and well-being were restored.
4. One needs not be religious to be in overwhelming wonder of the Bing bang, in absolute awe of both the order and the chaos on earth and in the universe, the enormous destructive and renewal processes that affect the earth and all its inhabitants.

Let's conclude that the animal and plant inhabitants on earth must eat to live and hence the food chain is not "bad" or "good." It is what it is – a sustaining requirement. We will quickly conclude that death is a requirement in that no renewed members of a species will be possible if the old members don't die.

Now we can get back to regulators. My favorite people. I don't want to bloviate about California's water problem. For one little fishy, they waste trillions of gallons of water. On the same day that they worry about the little fishy, numerous species are undergoing mutations, some of which will cause their demise.

My cowboy wisdom tells me that there are a lot of good people concerned with overfishing, inhumane killings of seals, excessive usage of pesticides, genetic modifications which could prove harmful, global climate change and I can continue with a long list of concerns. I won't. so, what do all these concerned good people do? They elect snake oil salesmen, DMV activists, old disheveled socialist fire brands, a whole array of dreamers who misunderstand that a bloated array of regulators are not Einsteins, Edisons and the ilk. They don't grasp the words "how much will it cost" and "when do you want it to happen."

By now, some of you [TTIII points at the audience] must think of me as some right-wing nut, "deplorable" and essentially "irredeemable." I assure you, I'm not any one of those. Even more, I'm not racist, homophobic, White supremacist and climate change denier. And every so often, I like, good heartedly, to mock the various brigades of "do gooders," I must confess that mocking these folks is mischievously enjoyable. Let me have some fun before I get serious. I'm treading on the light side because I want to tell you about my real war, World War IV, and that is not fun at all.

It is not difficult to mock the stupid ones. Examples abound.

1. A New England University should be sued for malpractice. The Cortess woman got an economics degree there. She has proven that the University accepted her even though she does not grasp arithmetic – a necessary prerequisite in the study of economics. "Ms. Cortess, you can't count trillions by using your toes, one at a time." The University paid $32,000 for a short speech delivered by Snooky, a South Jersey "Scholar" of bovine behavior by a humanoid.

2. The Washington Post declared Baghdady as an "Austere Islamic scholar," the bowwow who decided on this characterization of a devilish depraved humanoid cannot be considered as a person deserving any sympathy for certified idiots.
3. I was going to involve Trump in this trashing sector of my bloviation, but decided not to beyond the following:
    - There has never been a better swamp Drainer than Trump. Remember: "When you drain a swamp, don't wear a tuxedo, don't speak Shakespearean English – wear dirty clothes, speak dirty and don't accept incoming missiles without overwhelming retaliation." (I am solely responsible for this quote). I will wait for our narrator to present my WWIV tale.

Act III, Scene 2

NARRATOR: I find it interesting that a rancher from the "middle of nowhere, Arizona" keeps strongly hinting to us here that he wants to talk about World War IV ("WWIV").

Some people who have experienced any of the 20th Century wars or experienced their aftermath would recoil from the thought that another massive war is ongoing or coming soon for a visit. And yet, here you are, attempting to scare us to death.

TTIII: You are the history professor. You deal with the explanation of the "Why do major events happen?" Unlike you, I ponder more on the side of "what really happened?" I deal with simpler things; note the following:

1. In the last three World Wars – <u>the initiators of each war have decisively lost</u> – whether they stood in the "Winners Circle" or the "Losers Circle." I don't need to tell you the detail.

2. <u>The sole true "winner" was the U.S. The "real losers" were looted</u> (Germany, Austro-Hungarian Empire, the Ottoman Empire). Some, like the Ottoman Empire, have become a carcass for British/French "genius diplomats" to feed – creating a Middle East permanent battlefield war lasting already for more than 100 years.

3. In WWII, the same things happened. The "real losers" were completely devastated. The "presumed winners" began losing their empires and became economic basket cases.

4. <u>The sole true "winner" was the U.S.</u> which resuscitated both winners and losers. Stop for a moment and draw an interim

conclusion from just the facts. WWII was longer than WWI. It generated much more casualties. The weaponry was vastly more deadly. It had much more ideological underpinning – in your parlance, it was a real "war of civilizations" – Western democracy vs. Fascist totalitarians.

5. WWI, followed by a worldwide depression, followed by WWII and its massive devastation forced all players – winners and losers to clamor to establish some world order, to produce some security against massive atrocities.
6. It took just days from WWII's end to have WWIII commence. It took longer than the previous two combined (46 years). There were many more casualties, spread over more regions and countries. It was total war – economic, military, cultural and ideological. Newer and vastly more lethal weapons became available. Unimaginable threats could be made, and executed by evil regimes.
7. Last on this facts trip: The U.S. was again the sole real winner. It was 1991. This time, the U.S. got drunk with victory and forgot that another and still bigger was – WWIV – has begun. And now I'm ready to tell you about my cowboy-wisdom take on WWIV.

NARRATOR: I have patiently and with interest listened to your attempt to be a historian. As an aside, you did better than many academics in our colleges who besmirch the U.S., rewrite history and are advocates for bizarre ideological refuse.

I noticed that you desire to tell us the 'little things" that you think you know well AND WHICH ARE CONNECTED TO OUR TRIBUTE TO YOUR FATHER. You probably also want me to deal with the big and sweeping ideas regarding WWIV that will or could possibly make your views legitimate. Am I right?

TTIII: Yes, you are right.

NARRATOR: It is plausible to assume that WAR IS THE NORMAL STATE AFFLICTING HUMANS. PEACE IS A SHORT RESTING CONDITION TO POSSIBLY RECUPERATE FROM THE RAVAGES OF THE CONFLICTS.

This idea reminds me of a story I heard – I can't vouch for it – about this Oxford Don who was tired of wars and their aftermath. He wanted to shed his job and ignore, by being far away, the stupid, ignorant, deplorable right-wing fascists, mostly also homophobic and racist. He wanted to experience PEACE.

He moved to the Falkland Islands, off Argentina's east coast. There isn't much one can say about the Falkland Islands. It has a lousy climate. It is isolated and insulated from anything that might even approach having cultural events. For the good Don, it looked like a hospice that will calm him on the way to heaven.

The Falkland Islands were British Territory, a remnant of its "glorious Imperial past." Argentinean generals decided to grab this sorry little piece of real estate which had nothing of value – minerals, strategic location, etc. – one couldn't even have a decent military parade there and display all the medals one never deserved and wear the fancy uniforms (almost as fancy as doormen wear in luxury hotels in New York. London and Paris) that fit so well and attracted the ladies. In 1982, the British Prime Minister ("The Iron Lady," Thatcher) engaged Argentina in a two-month modern war and protected "vital British interests."

The good Don was saved. Used the time to write a book and returned to his beloved Oxford.

- "There is no place to hide from war," he murmured to himself.

Let me try another earth-shaking wise statement. A short little tale precedes it. When WWIII began in late 1945, there were two superpowers, clearly on a collision course, replacing the older empires. Both powers were preparing for a prolonged total war. It did last 46 years. For reasons we have already discussed, THE SOVIET UNION CRUMBLED IN 1991.

A very bright U.S. State Department functionary wrote a book "The End of History" ruminating about a world that has only one colossus power, military and economic. The U.S. exhibited all the symptoms of "drunkenness," given the immense victory. The tendency was to disarm militarily, "Thinking Big" Globally, allowing multinational bodies handle global problems – security, economic development, health, trade and everything else of importance. This tendency was not new. It has been prevalent before the WWIII victory.

Throughout World War III, all major geopolitical players attempted, overtly and covertly, to reduce the economic power of the U.S. one of these attempts is especially important.

In October 1973, Saudi Arabia, being a key player in the OPEC cartel, had managed to maneuver OPEC to QUADRUPLE THE OIL PRICES in a very short time frame. It provided a unique shock to the entire world.

- You don't need many explanations and pedantic treatment of MidEast history. Just remember that: "OPEC SIGNED ITS DEATH CERTIFICATE THEN AND THERE."
  As an extra bonus to remembering the above, consider:
- "The foot you step on today, maybe connected to the ass you kiss tomorrow." Saudi Arabia today requires strong U.S. support for the regime that attempted to knock U.S. down a few notches (economically).

There are additional extra bonuses for the U.S. that derive from OPEC's falling from grace:

- The U.S. achieved energy independence due to its technology development spurred by the insane price hike.
- Most of the MidEast rogue regimes have had their arrogance (geopolitically) curtailed.

One more attempt at geopolitical economics won't hurt a rancher like you. Let's touch on Europe's soft spot, Climate hypochondria. The points I want to make are ALL ECONOMICS – NO SCIENCE ARGUMENT. THIS IS A TOUGH ONE.

- Without touching the substance of the climate change debate, it is quite unarguably clear that: <u>Two attempts had been made to bankrupt the U.S. via the climate hypochondria – All in the open</u>. The first was the Kyoto Agreement (1997 Treaty). The burden of carbon emissions reduction was to be borne by developed countries to an extent that will drive many of them to bankruptcy. The Doha and Paris Agreements were aimed at the same objective.

[TTIII signals to the Narrator, he wishes to interrupt him.]

<u>TTIII</u>: Not being as learned as you are, I'll leave you to draw conclusions from your factual stories' recital. Let me tell you what I mean by WWIV. It isn't at all too complicated. Winning WWIII, did not eliminate a whole array of serious threats to me, my family and my country. My ranch is quite close to the Mexican border. This border is porous.

- The direct threat to my family is the large number of illegal border crossers pass my land. I don't wish to touch the "comprehensive solution to the immigration issues." <u>Until the number of illegals crossing my land goes to zero – I am at war – WWIV</u>.
  I'm totally open to be very generous with people who choose to use legal entry to the U.S.
- To all those who suggest that since I cannot tolerate the current level of illegals on my land that I could move somewhere else.
  This is a cruel suggestion, <u>I can't sell the ranch for peanuts</u> – thus, please stop the thought.
- The threat to my family can be somewhat controlled if, and only if, the illegals were simply people who are looking for work in the U.S. (In

the old days, this was the case.) Many are. But, a vast number are more than just people seeking a job. My enemies in this war are very clearly defined.

1. It is a criminal consortium in Mexico engaged in highly profitable lines of business.
    - Smuggling extremely potent drugs
    - Human traffic
    - Distribution networks of drugs in the U.S.
2. It is the CRIMINAL GOVERNMENTS in Central America most fitting the biblical saying – "Lands that devour their people."

- To all those who advocate a "Marshall Plan" type of "investment" in the criminal lands and whose hearts seriously bleed for the victims – work hard to stop giving the criminal thugs any money – the thugs will steal it all in a blink of any eye (my father loved to say "augenblik"). I stick with this partial classification of my enemies. You can worry about the "big picture" – Russia, China, Iran, North Korea and God only knows who else.

NARRATOR: How is knowing your views of your specific enemies related at all to your father? – It is still interesting to know your thought.

TTIII: I neglected to tell you that I was always aware of father's interest in the "big picture." I would like you to tell us all here: What is your view of America's enemies in this WWIV?

NARRATOR: I think that your question presupposes that we are actually today involved in WWIV. Well, rest assured that a massive WWIV is now in progress.

- This war is the largest war ever by many metrics. The casualties are suffered every day, and are likely to continue for decades.

This war has multiple ideological groups/blocs/alliances. We will just enumerate a few. The first grouping includes:

1. <u>Debris of the former Soviet Union</u>
   - This includes an authoritarian Russia.
   - A collection of authoritarian states – many with names ending with "stan."
   - A collection of former Russian surrogates – includes Cuba, Belarus, Nicaragua and other Central American dictatorships.
2. <u>Newcomers to Communist Ideology</u>, such as:
   - South Africa
   - Venezuela
3. <u>Plain old Fascists</u>
   - Multiple South American countries
   - Several Southeast Asian countries (e.g. Cambodia).

The above, collectively, are the debris of three world wars of the 20th Century.

The loose bond among the above groups is a deep – somewhat deranged view of the U.S. which has never been Colonial and imperialist and yet, tagged by these "enlightened" regimes with the not-so-appealing labels.

My "big picture" postulates that <u>your enemies are supported and encouraged</u> by the ones I will talk about.

- Think "Economics" (Primarily) when dealing with major events. An unwritten strong alliance exists aimed at seriously hurting the U.S. economy. Consider the various members of this alliance.
  - It is Chinese production of super opioids that floods our southern porous borders. The same cartels you consider as enemies smooth the way for the drugs that seriously hurt the U.S. THERE ARE MANY OTHER THINGS THAT CHINA DOES IN THE ECONOMICS ARENA. It ranges from stealing technology, manipulating currency, methodically acquiring control of major operating ports worldwide, etc.
  - It is the Russians, unable to swallow WWIII loss who are aiming to disrupt any and all U.S. alliances – some disruptions with considerable success, particularly via shenanigans in the U.N. (the pretend "World government") and international bodies. It is easy to notice the closeness of Russia/China cooperation when disrupting the U.S. These disruptions are costly to the U.S. and are a clear and present danger to us.
  For decades, the U.S. was the sheriff protecting key choke points to enable protecting world trade routes (Suez and Panama Canals, multiple straits – such as the straits of Hurmuz, the Bosporus, Gibraltar, etc.). Consider: Russia and China have enabled Iran to seriously endanger oil/gas supplies – making the costs of defense prohibitive.
  This "disrupt America's economy" loose alliance has strange bedfellows coagulating policies with Russia or China, and many times, with both.

- It is almost comical and sad to consider who these strange bedfellows are. First, think of the really bad apples. It is <u>North Korea, a deranged country</u>, which has the means to do enormously bad things, that actually forces <u>inordinacy cost of defense</u> borne by the U.S, Japan and South Korea.

    <u>It is Iran</u> which will undoubtedly acquire the bomb. If it does, it will cause drastic changes in the MidEast.

    <u>It is Pakistan</u> who has the bomb and is strapped for cash, that might partner with North Korea and Iran in one happy <u>nuclear bazaar</u>, making it easy for any two-bit tyrant to acquire a bomb or two.

    <u>It is the European Union</u> ("EU"), originally designed as an Orwellian "third force" in the world of U.S and Russia superpower competition, that provided an enormous burden on the U.S. economy by repeatedly worshipping its sainthood re: climate change. The cost of U.S. subscription to this religion is prohibitive – <u>given that the U.S. is expected to shoulder the lion's share of the cost</u>.

    <u>It is the smart terrorists</u> who have learned that stupid lone wolf attacks gets you only good television, but economic disruptions to the U.S. gets America to bleed, slowly and surely to weaken the enormous colossus. Using the multiple rogue and failed states on this planet, with low cost and effort leads to huge defensive outlays.

Act III, Scene 3

TTIII: I get your view that WWIV has an important and overriding economic factor. The enemy, whoever he is, wants to see the U.S. bankrupt first.

NARRATOR: You got this one right. Your father knew two true enemies. He saw the fascist totalitarians defeated in his midlife. He saw the pretend utopian Communist theology defeated at the end of his life – what he didn't see, but had an inkling of it, that the two ideologies didn't die yet. (Really die …). It is this inkling that grants him a medal of honor.

He also knew, that the economic conflicts are not the only elements of WWIV. Major conflicts always require an ideological umbrella. He did not know, nor appreciate sufficiently even if he knew, the power of religious fanaticism.

One such group of fanatics – has used its Islamic fanaticism to develop terrorism as an art form and a technology to provide an incredible threat to humanity on this planet.

The religious fanaticism has two strains. The least problematic is the deranged strain. The one that calls for homicide vests to be used to kill infidels anywhere. This strain also calls to destroy Buddha statues with canon shots, behead people who would not convert to Islam and use obnoxious/barbaric means to intimidate infidels. The other strain, the more sophisticated one, expects to acquire weapons and technology that might force infidels to behave in a dictated way.

Finally, and more importantly, your father knew with certainty, the obnoxious European capacity to appease their enemies. And hence, encourage the deranged, and even the more sane of their enemies, to behave without fear of dire consequences to their villainy.

It is this knowledge that made his worldview most pessimistic.

[A tall man appears from the back stage. The Narrator recognizes him and waves to him.]

NARRATOR: I'm pleased to see Robert Barr. I met Robert at the ranch several times in the 1960's and 1970's. I'm assuming that you've heard the tribute to TTII proceedings from back stage. I wondered why you haven't joined us sooner. I know, however, that in spite of your respect for TTII accomplishments, you don't like many of the opinions you heard about him, his views and the tributes we paid to his actions and beliefs.

ROBERT: I'm respectful of good old TTII. This said, I don't want to rain on the parade here. TTIII claimed that he is just a simple rancher. I'm a simple academic, science bent. I don't come from the east or west coasts. I'm a Texan from El Paso – just across crime-riddled Juarez, Mexico. My views differ significantly from those I heard here. I'm looking for an opportunity to air the much less pessimistic views I hold.

NARRATOR: I'm looking forward to see you tomorrow. The objectives on my mind: (1) hear some challenges to views expressed here and, AVOID THINGS/THOUGHTS LEFT JUST HANGING – WE MUST GET AN IDEA ON HOW TO WIN WWIV.

Made in the USA
Columbia, SC
21 May 2023